Better Homes and Gardens®
Candy

BETTER HOMES AND GARDENS® BOOKS
Editor: Gerald M. Knox
Art Director: Ernest Shelton
Managing Editor: David A. Kirchner

Food and Nutrition Editor: Nancy Byal
Department Head—Cook Books: Sharyl Heiken
Associate Department Heads: Sandra Granseth,
    Rosemary C. Hutchinson, Elizabeth Woolever
Senior Food Editors: Julie Henderson, Julia Malloy,
    Marcia Stanley
Associate Food Editors: Jill Burmeister, Molly Culbertson,
    Linda Foley, Linda Henry, Lynn Hoppe, Mary Jo Plutt,
    Maureen Powers, Joyce Trollope
Recipe Development Editor: Marion Viall
Test Kitchen Director: Sharon Stilwell
Test Kitchen Home Economists: Jean Brekke, Kay Cargill,
    Marilyn Cornelius, Maryellyn Krantz, Lynelle Munn,
    Dianna Nolin, Marge Steenson, Cynthia Volcko

Associate Art Directors: Linda Ford Vermie,
    Neoma Alt West, Randall Yontz
Copy and Production Editors: Marsha Jahns,
    Mary Helen Schiltz, Carl Voss, David A. Walsh
Assistant Art Directors: Harijs Priekulis, Tom Wegner
Senior Graphic Designers: Alisann Dixon,
    Lynda Haupert, Lyne Neymeyer
Graphic Designers: Mike Burns, Mike Eagleton,
    Deb Miner, Stan Sams, D. Greg Thompson,
    Darla Whipple, Paul Zimmerman

Vice President, Editorial Director: Doris Eby
Executive Director, Editorial Services: Duane L. Gregg

General Manager: Fred Stines
Director of Publishing: Robert B. Nelson
Vice President, Retail Marketing: Jamie Martin
Vice President, Direct Marketing: Arthur Heydendael

CANDY
Editors: Linda Henry, Mary Jo Plutt
Copy and Production Editor: Marsha Jahns
Graphic Designer: Mike Burns
Electronic Text Processor: Joyce Wasson

On the cover: *Fancy Liqueur Chocolates, Old-Time Fudge, Black Walnut Nougat, Peanut Brittle, Pinwheel Divinity, Cinnamon Gumdrops, Caramel Snappers, Caramel Pecan Logs,* and *Microwave Peanut Clusters.* (See Index for recipe page numbers.)

Our seal assures you that every recipe in *Candy* has been tested by the Better Homes and Gardens® Test Kitchen. This means that each recipe is practical and reliable, and meets our high standards of taste appeal.

Our fondness for sweets seems to come naturally, and candy is probably the most popular sweet! Through the ages, candy has been used as an expression of love, and no gift is savored more than homemade candy.

Some homemade candies are simple to make and fun for even the novice candy-maker. Others require total concentration and effort in their preparation. This book offers you a sampling of both.

Before you get started, though, be sure to review the first chapter, "Candy Basics," which contains the hows and whys of candy-making. After you have familiarized yourself with the basics, turn to the classic, the specialty, and the short and snappy recipe sections. You'll find everything from Opera Fudge to Glazed Almonds to Caramel Snappers. No matter which recipe you choose, you'll find each step thoroughly explained to ensure success.

CANDY BASICS

What do you need to know to become a first-rate candy-maker? You'll find it all right here. We'll tell you how to get started, what equipment you'll need, and why candy mixtures behave as they do. Special sections feature several different candy-making techniques, such as beating fudge, pulling taffy, and dipping candy. We'll even explain how to store candy to make sure it stays fresh.

Step-by-step photos and directions guide you through unfamiliar techniques so that your candy is sure to turn out right time after time.

Before you begin

Although it's important to read and thoroughly understand any recipe before you begin, with candy recipes, it is *essential*.

Start by reading the recipe through and noting (1) what equipment is needed, (2) how much attention is required, (3) how long it will take to cook, and (4) if any cooling, beating, and/or drying time is required. Be sure to use the proper equipment (see pages 8 and 9) and allow plenty of time to prepare the recipe successfully. Don't be fooled into thinking that a short recipe is necessarily going to take little effort or be fast to prepare.

Next, assemble all of the equipment you'll need and measure all of the ingredients. For example, have the walnuts chopped before the fudge recipe says to beat them in. The time it takes to chop the nuts is too long for the fudge to sit idle.

Measure accurately, and don't make substitutions for basic ingredients. *Never* alter quantities in candy recipes. Do not halve or double recipes; the proportions have been worked out for the recipes as they are printed. The only safe way to double your yield for a specific recipe is to make two separate batches.

Consider the humidity

Humidity affects the preparation of all candies, so avoid making candy on very humid days. Humidity affects the preparation of divinity and nougat to such an extent that you should plan to make these two candies on a relatively dry day. If the day is humid, no amount of beating will make these two candies set up.

Cooking procedures

The first step we recommend when cooking most candy mixtures is to butter the sides of the saucepan. This helps prevent the mixture from climbing the sides of the pan and boiling over.

Usually, the next step is to combine the sugar with the other ingredients and bring the mixture to boiling. It's very important to dissolve the sugar entirely during this step.

As you cook the mixture to dissolve the sugar, stir it constantly, but gently, so it doesn't splash on the sides of

the saucepan. This precaution helps prevent sugar crystals from forming and clumping together in the saucepan.

If some of the candy mixture splashes on the side of the saucepan, cover the pan and cook for 30 to 45 seconds. As the steam condenses, it will dissolve any crystals that may have formed. Watch carefully, though, so that the candy mixture doesn't boil over. (Candy mixtures using milk products or molasses should not be covered; they foam if steam cannot escape, and may boil over.)

After the sugar is dissolved, carefully clip the candy thermometer to the side of the saucepan. (Always check the thermometer's accuracy before you begin. See page 8.) For an accurate reading, be sure that the bulb of the candy thermometer is completely covered with boiling liquid, not just with foam, and that it does not touch the bottom of the pan. Always read the thermometer at eye level.

When cooking candy mixtures, it is extremely important to keep the mixture boiling at a moderate, steady rate over the entire surface (see page 10). Throughout our recipes we suggest rangetop temperatures for cooking the candy mixtures. If you use this information as a guide, you'll be able to maintain the best rate of cooking for optimum results. Because every rangetop heats differently, however, you also will have to rely on knowledge of your rangetop to judge whether you'll need to use a slightly higher or lower temperature to cook the candy mixture within the recommended time.

Understanding sugar mixtures

Candy-making depends ultimately upon the transformation of sugar and liquids into syrups. Learning how to cook these sugar-liquid mixtures is the key to successful candy-making.

Sugar-liquid mixtures change character as they increase in temperature, so the final temperature to which a mixture is cooked has a definite effect on the finished candy. Mixtures boiled to relatively low final temperatures yield soft candies such as fudge; mixtures boiled to very high final temperatures produce hard candies such as brittles. Mixtures cooked to temperatures in between produce caramels, taffies, and divinity.

Candy-Making Equipment

Using the right equipment can help assure that your candy-making efforts will be a success.

Saucepans

A high quality, heavy aluminum saucepan is the best choice for making candy. Aluminum pans conduct heat very evenly. Other types of metal pans, such as stainless steel, require careful watching because they may have hot spots and not heat evenly.

Using the correct size pan is equally important. A pan that's too small to hold the candy mixture can lead to messy and dangerous boil-overs. A pan that's too large can result in inaccurate thermometer readings, because the candy mixture will not cover the bulb of the candy thermometer. During our testing, we tried various pan sizes, and have recommended the best size for each recipe.

When melting dipping chocolate, temperature control is critical, so it's wise to use a double boiler. This keeps the chocolate away from the direct heat (see dipping instructions on pages 18 and 19).

Candy thermometers

Cooking candy mixtures to the correct temperature is a very critical part of candy-making. A candy thermometer is an indispensable item because it takes the guesswork out of testing candy mixtures.

When choosing a candy thermometer, look for one that is clearly marked and easy to read. Choose a thermometer with a mercury bulb that's set low enough to measure the heat in the syrup, but won't touch the bottom of the pan. And look for a thermometer with a clip that attaches to the pan. Candy thermometers are available in department and hardware stores, kitchen supply stores, and some large supermarkets.

Before *every* use, check the accuracy of the thermometer. To do this, place the candy thermometer in a saucepan of boiling water for a few minutes and then read the temperature. If the thermometer registers above or below 212°, add or subtract the same number of degrees from the recipe temperature, and cook to that temperature.

For example, if the thermometer reads 210°, cook the candy 2 degrees *lower* than the recipe temperature. If the thermometer reads 214°, cook the candy 2 degrees *higher* than the recipe states. Checking the candy thermometer allows you to make adjustments for any inaccuracy and for weather-related factors.

After removing the candy thermometer from a hot candy mixture, immerse it in hot water. This will protect the thermometer from a sudden temperature change and will make it easier to clean later.

Using a candy thermometer is the most accurate way to test candy mixtures, but it's not the only way. Other testing methods are explained on pages 10 and 11.

Beating equipment

A wooden spoon with a long handle is ideal for stirring candy mixtures as they cook, because the spoon never becomes too hot to handle.

And it's also the best tool for beating fudge and penuche (*do not* use an electric mixer because the mixture will overtax the mixer motor).

Unlike fudge, divinity and nougat require a sturdy, freestanding electric mixer. When you're beating either of these candy mixtures, the denseness of the mixture strains the motor of a mixer. Portable mixers and some freestanding mixers simply don't have enough power to handle these candy mixtures. And because of the strain on the motor, it is not a good idea to make consecutive batches of divinity or nougat.

Large platters or marble slabs
You will need a large surface for working with hot candy mixtures, such as taffies and fondants. Marble slabs work well because they're heavy and smooth, and the cold surface cools the candy rapidly. But you also may use a large platter. Be sure, however, that the platter has a rim around the perimeter, or the candy mixture will flow off the platter as quickly as you pour it on! (If you use a marble slab, cooling times may be shorter than the times suggested in our recipes.)

Special equipment
Kitchen and candy-making supply stores carry a lot of special candy-making equipment.

Paper candy cups, available in many colors, can add eye appeal to homemade dipped candies.

For molding candies, individual plastic and metal molds and sheet molds are available. Also available are sheet molds especially made to withstand the high temperatures of hard candy mixtures.

Candy-dipping forks, designed with a looped tip, are handy when dipping centers into chocolate. However, an ordinary table fork, a meat fork, or a fondue fork may work equally well.

Wooden candy paddles or spatulas are useful when working fondant because of their broad base, but a wooden spoon also can do the job.

Microwave recipes
The microwave recipes included in this book were tested in 600- to 700-watt microwave ovens. If the wattage for your oven is different, use the manufacturer's directions as a guide.

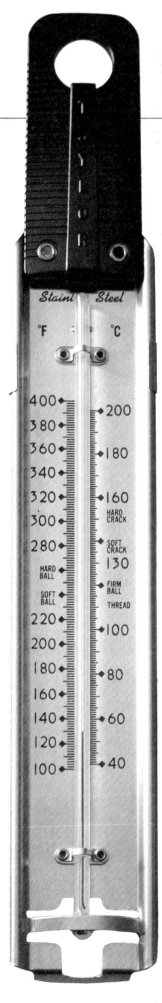

Boiling and Testing Candy Mixtures

Cooking candy at the proper rate and then accurately determining when it is "done" are two very important steps when making candy.

Boiling candy mixtures

Candy mixtures should boil at a moderate, steady rate over the entire surface (see photos below). As a guide, in our recipes we have suggested rangetop temperatures for cooking the candy mixtures. Because every rangetop cooks differently, however, you may have to use slightly higher or lower temperatures than those suggested in order to maintain the best rate of cooking and to cook the candy mixtures within the recommended times. Cooking too fast or too slowly will cause the texture of the candy to become too hard or too soft.

Use extra caution when boiling mixtures that contain dairy products. These candies have a tendency to stick to the bottom of the pan, and if boiled too hard over too-high heat, they will scorch and may even curdle.

Testing candy mixtures

You can count on the most accurate results if you use a candy thermometer. If a thermometer is not available, however, test candy mixtures by using the cold water test.

Test the candy shortly before it reaches the suggested minimum cooking time in the recipe. Working quickly, drop a few drops of the hot mixture from a spoon into a cup of very cold (but not icy) water. Working in the water, use your fingers to form the drops of candy into a ball. Remove the ball from the water. The firmness of the ball will indicate the temperature of the mixture (see photos opposite).

If the mixture has not reached the correct stage, continue cooking it for another 2 to 3 minutes. Then, quickly retest the candy, using fresh water and a clean spoon for the test. Continue cooking and retesting till the desired stage is reached.

Even if candies are similar and are cooked to the same stage, the final temperatures may vary. For example, some fudge mixtures will reach soft-ball stage at 234° and others at 240°. The temperature difference is caused by the ingredients added to the basic sugar mixture. For best results, always cook to the precise temperature recommended in the recipe.

Boiling candy mixtures
Boil all candy mixtures, including this divinity, at a moderate, steady rate over the entire surface.

Foaming will occur in candy mixtures that contain dairy products, such as this fudge.

For an accurate reading, be sure the bulb of the thermometer is covered with boiling liquid, not just foam.

Thread stage (230°-233°)
Dip a teaspoon into the pan of hot candy mixture. When you remove the spoon, the mixture will fall off in a 2-inch fine, thin thread.

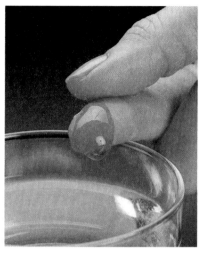

Soft-ball stage (234°-240°)
Shape drops of candy into a ball in the cold water. When the ball is removed from the water, it will *immediately* flatten and run between your fingers.

Firm-ball stage (244°-248°)
Shape drops of candy into a ball in the cold water. When ball is removed from the water, it will be firm enough to hold its shape, but quickly flatten at room temperature.

Hard-ball stage (250°-266°)
Shape drops of candy into a ball in the cold water. When ball is removed from the water, it can be deformed by pressure, but will not flatten.

Soft-crack stage (270°-290°)
When dropped into cold water, the candy mixture will separate into hard, but pliable and elastic, threads.

Hard-crack stage (295°-310°)
When dropped into cold water, the candy mixture will separate into hard, brittle threads that snap easily.

Beating Candy Mixtures

Taffies, which require pulling, and fondants, which require kneading, aren't the only candies that need to be worked with your hands or a utensil to develop the proper end product. In the case of fudge and pralines, manual beating with a wooden spoon brings about a change in appearance and texture. With divinity and nougat, beating with a sturdy, freestanding electric mixer transforms two very different mixtures (beaten egg whites and hot syrup) into candy.

Beating candy with a wooden spoon

Always prepare your pan or have the waxed paper ready before beginning to beat fudge or pralines because the candies can thicken during the beating process in what will seem like record time. If you stop to prepare the pan or even tear off a piece of waxed paper, you may not get the candy mixture out of the saucepan!

Fudge and pralines are cooked to a specific temperature, cooled to a lower temperature, and then beaten. When you first begin to beat either of these candy mixtures, they will be quite thin and very glossy. As the beating continues, the mixtures begin to thicken; this is the time to stir in nuts or other ingredients. At this point, watch very carefully as the mixture continues to thicken and the gloss *just starts* to disappear. When this stage is reached, quickly turn fudge into the prepared pan or drop pralines onto the waxed paper.

Beating candy with a sturdy, freestanding electric mixer

When making divinity or nougat, timing is very important.

Separate the eggs, but *do not* begin beating the egg whites before you start cooking the candy mixture. (If you do, the egg whites will revert to a liquid state and cannot be beaten again.) *Immediately* after the sugar mixture has cooked to the recommended temperature, remove it from the heat; then begin beating the egg whites till stiff peaks form.

Pour the hot candy mixture over the stiffly beaten egg whites in a slow, steady stream (slightly less than ⅛-inch diameter) to ensure proper blending. At first, as the hot candy mixture hits the cooler egg whites, it may become hard. Continue beating and scraping the bowl occasionally, and the mixture will soften.

For divinity, continue beating till the candy just starts to lose its gloss. The mixture should fall in a ribbon off the beaters. It should mound on itself and not disappear into the mixture in the bowl.

For nougat, beat till the candy becomes very thick and less glossy. When the beaters are lifted, the mixture should fall in a ribbon that mounds on itself, then slowly disappears into the remaining mixture.

1 Beating fudge
The mixture will be thin and very glossy when you begin beating. Beat vigorously with a wooden spoon till fudge just begins to thicken; stir in nuts or other ingredients.

2 Continue beating the fudge till it becomes very thick and *just starts* to lose its gloss. At this point, quickly turn the fudge into the prepared pan.

1 Beating divinity
Gradually pour the hot mixture in a thin stream (less than ⅛-inch diameter) over egg whites, beating with electric mixer on high speed.

2 When the candy just starts to lose its gloss, lift the beaters. The mixture should fall in a ribbon that mounds on itself but does not disappear into the remaining mixture.

Pulling Taffy and Kneading Fondant

Although most candies are beaten with wooden spoons or electric mixers, the thick taffy mixture is pulled with buttered hands till the right consistency is reached.

After a taffy mixture is cooked to the recommended temperature (which in our recipes is 265°, hard-ball stage), pour it out of the saucepan and onto a platter or marble slab, or into a buttered baking pan. Allow the mixture to cool just enough so that it can be handled easily. (Put the platter or baking pan on a cooling rack to speed the cooling process, if you wish.) Check the hot taffy mixture cautiously to guard against burns. It may be cool on the surface, but extremely hot underneath, so gather up the taffy mixture carefully.

With buttered hands, begin pulling, folding, and twisting the taffy mixture till it turns a creamy color and is stiff and quite difficult to pull. For our recipes, this should take about 10 minutes. However, this timing will depend on several factors: (1) the temperature of the candy, (2) the room temperature, and (3) the speed at which the candy is pulled. During this pulling process, the air that is incorporated into the candy reduces the intensity of the color, and gives the candy a lighter texture.

The candy is ready to snip when the end cracks off as the candy is tapped against a work surface. Divide the pulled candy into fourths and twist and pull each piece into a long strand about ½ inch

1 Pulling taffy
With buttered hands, carefully work the warm taffy mixture into a ball. If you have helpers, divide the taffy mixture among them. Then, pull, fold, and twist the taffy mixture, as shown.

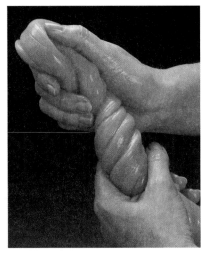

2 As you pull the taffy mixture, air is incorporated into the candy and changes the color from an intense shade to a more creamy color.

Pulling, folding, and twisting the taffy helps to improve its texture.

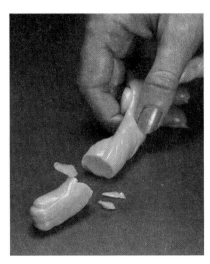

3 Cracking taffy
Work the candy till it becomes difficult to pull. Tap it on your work surface; if it cracks, it is ready to snip.

Divide candy into fourths; twist and pull into long strands about ½ inch thick. Snip into bite-size pieces.

thick. Use buttered scissors to snip each strand of taffy into bite-size pieces.

Wrap each piece of taffy in clear plastic wrap to prevent it from becoming soft and sticky during storage. Wrapping the individual pieces also prevents them from sticking to one another.

Kneading Fondant

The primary objective in fondant-making is to work the candy into a smooth, creamy mass.

After the candy mixture is cooked to 240° (soft-ball stage), carefully pour the mixture out of the saucepan and onto a platter or marble slab. *Do not scrape the saucepan.*

Allow the mixture to stand, undisturbed, till it is slightly warm to the touch. Then begin working the fondant mixture with a wooden spoon or paddle by scraping the mixture from the edge of the platter or marble slab toward the center. When you begin, the fondant mixture will be very thick and translucent. Continue working the fondant till it becomes creamy, opaque, and stiff. You'll need to work the fondant mixture about 10 minutes.

Gather the fondant into a ball and knead it till it's smooth and free of lumps. This should take about 5 minutes. Wrap the fondant in clear plastic wrap and let it stand (ripen) at room temperature for 24 hours. This ripening is necessary for smooth, creamy, and pliable fondant.

1 Working fondant
Cool the fondant mixture, without stirring, till it's slightly warm to the touch.

Using a wooden spoon or paddle, begin to scrape the edges of the fondant mixture into the center of the large platter or marble slab.

2 Keep working the fondant till it becomes white and firm, which will take about 10 minutes. Turn the platter occasionally, always scraping the candy that's around the edges back toward the center of the platter. You may need to use both hands as the mixture stiffens.

3 Gather the fondant into a ball and knead it in your hands till it's smooth and free of lumps.

Knead the fondant by turning and folding the candy mixture continuously in your hands.

15

Molding Candy

Molding candy can be as simple as pouring leftover dipping chocolate into molds, as elaborate as creating filled chocolate cups, or as elegant as molding individual pieces of fudge.

Plastic sheet molds

Flexible, plastic sheet molds can turn candy into all sorts of fun and fancy shapes. These molds can be filled with melted chocolate, various colors of confectioner's coatings, or even fudge.

The molds must be clean and dry before filling. Greasing is not necessary when you're filling the molds with melted chocolate or confectioner's coating, and could ruin the appearance of the finished candy. However, if molding fudge, lightly oiling the molds will make it easier to release the fudge from the molds.

When molding melted chocolate or confectioner's coating, spoon the melted mixture into all the cavities in the mold. If necessary, use a spatula to spread it evenly in the cavities. Tap mold gently several times on a countertop to remove air bubbles. You may need to use a wooden pick to remove any air bubbles on the surface of the candy.

Chill the mold till the candy has hardened. To unmold, invert; gently flex or tap the mold and the candies will fall out.

Molds for hard candies

These plastic sheet molds are similar to the molds mentioned above, but are made of a heavier plastic designed to withstand the heat of hard candies.

To use the molds, lightly oil them; then pour the hot candy mixture into them. Tap the molds to remove air bubbles. Let the candy stand about 10 minutes or till firm. Invert the molds and twist till the candies come out.

Lollipop molds

These molds are available in both types of plastic, so you can have chocolate lollipops or hard candy lollipops! Fill the cavities in the mold; tap the mold to remove any air bubbles. Slide a lollipop stick into the indentation in each cavity. Chill the melted chocolate molds till they are firm, or allow the hard candy molds to stand at room temperature till firm. Unmold by carefully lifting the stick and candy out of the cavity.

Metal molds

Small, decorative metal molds can be used to mold candies in much the same way as the plastic sheet molds. Or, they can be used to create beautifully shaped individual pieces of fudge.

To make molded chocolates, pour the melted chocolate or confectioner's coating into the molds. Chill till chocolate is firm; invert and tap the mold against the countertop to release the chocolate from the mold.

To make molded pieces of fudge, lightly oil the molds. Working quickly, press the fudge into the molds with your fingers. Unmold by using wooden picks to loosen the fudge from the corners of the mold; invert onto a clean, dry surface. Let the fudge stand about 20 minutes or till it is firm.

Three-dimensional molds

Both plastic and metal three-dimensional molds are available. To make hollow or solid candies, follow the directions that come with the molds.

Care of molds

Wash plastic candy molds in warm water; dry. Do not wash the molds with soap or detergent, or in dishwashers, because the molds eventually may dry out and crack.

Wash metal molds in hot, soapy water.

Using plastic sheet molds
To unmold the candies, invert the mold about an inch above a clean, dry surface. Gently flex or tap the mold; the candy will fall out.

1 Using individual metal molds
Lightly oil small individual metal molds. Use your fingers to press the fudge into the molds.

2 To remove the fudge from the metal molds, use a wooden pick to loosen the corners. Invert the molds onto a clean, dry surface. Let the fudge stand till firm.

1 Making filled chocolate cups
With a small paintbrush, brush melted chocolate onto the bottom and up the sides of paper candy cups till about ⅛ inch thick. Chill or freeze till hardened.

2 Place a small amount of melted *fondant* into each hardened chocolate cup. (Cool fondant slightly or it could melt the chocolate.)
  Carefully place a halved and well-drained *maraschino cherry* on top of the fondant.

3 To seal the chocolate cups, spoon another layer of melted chocolate over the maraschino cherry halves. Chill or freeze till hardened.
  To serve, peel paper cups away from chocolate cups.

Dipping Candy

There's no mystique to dipping candy. As you read through the information on these two pages, you'll find that dipping candy can be as simple as covering pretzels, fresh fruits, marshmallows, or even animal crackers (see opposite page) with melted chocolate or confectioner's coating, or it can be as elaborate as making luscious candy-store favorites.

Types of chocolate
We recommend three types of chocolate products for dipping. In order to differentiate between these chocolate products, each product must contain certain percentages of key ingredients, as set by the Food and Drug Administration (FDA).
● Semisweet chocolate contains at least 35 percent chocolate liquor (a liquid paste extracted from the cocoa bean), additional cocoa butter (a vegetable fat obtained from the cocoa bean), and sugar.
● Milk chocolate contains at least 10 percent chocolate liquor, 12 percent whole milk solids, and additional cocoa butter.

Both products are available as chocolate pieces, in block form, or in round disks.
● Confectioner's coating is a general term used for a variety of chocolatelike products. Most of the cocoa butter has been removed and replaced by another vegetable fat. Vanilla, vanillin, or other flavors, plus vegetable coloring, frequently are added to confectioner's coating.

Confectioner's coating is sometimes called white chocolate, almond bark, or summer coating. Available in block form or round disks, many candy-makers prefer to use confectioner's coating instead of chocolate for dipping because the confectioner's coating does not require tempering; simply chop and melt it.

Tempering chocolate
The phrase "tempering chocolate" refers to the process of melting and cooling chocolate to the correct dipping temperature.

As chocolate melts, the cocoa butter separates from the chocolate liquor. Then, as the mixture cools, the cocoa butter blends evenly back into the chocolate liquor. Without tempering, the surface of the chocolate will speckle or develop gray streaks as it hardens. Known as "blooming," this affects only the appearance, not the quality or flavor.

Dip chocolates on a cool, dry day (60° to 65°). Use 1 to 1½ pounds of chocolate for dipping to ensure maximum coverage of centers. (More than 2 pounds is difficult to keep evenly melted during the dipping process.)

Finely chop the chocolate so it will melt quickly and evenly. Place water in bottom of a double boiler to within ½ inch of the upper pan. Make sure the upper pan does not touch the water, or the chocolate could be overheated. Bring water to boiling; remove from heat. Place about *one-fourth* of the chocolate in top of double boiler; set over hot water till chocolate begins to melt. Add remaining chocolate, about ½ cup at a time, *stirring constantly* after each addition till melted. Stir till chocolate reaches 120°.

If necessary to help chocolate reach 120°, reheat water. To reheat water, remove upper pan of chocolate. Bring water to boiling; remove from heat. Then place upper pan over hot water again. (Use care not to let any water fall into the chocolate, or chocolate will thicken and be ruined.)

After chocolate has reached 120°, refill bottom of the double boiler with *cool* water to within ½ inch of the upper pan. Place chocolate over cool water. *Stir frequently* till the chocolate cools to 83°. This should take about 30 minutes.

Follow the directions, opposite, for dipping centers. Work quickly, stirring chocolate frequently to keep it evenly heated. Chocolate will stay close to dipping temperature (83°) about 30 minutes. If chocolate cools to below 80°, you will need to retemper it.

1 Dipping centers
Drop centers, one at a time, into melted chocolate or confectioner's coating; turn to coat. Lift center out; draw fork across rim of pan to remove excess chocolate.

2 Invert onto a baking sheet lined with waxed paper. Twist fork slightly as candy falls so you can swirl the top. (If a lot of chocolate pools at base, next time let more chocolate drip off fork.)

Wrapping and Storing Candy

Freshness is one reason people enjoy making homemade candy. And the secret to keeping candy fresh is proper storage.

Short-term storage

Most candies will keep well for two to three weeks if stored tightly covered in a cool, dry place.

It's best to avoid storing different types of candy together in the same container because hard candies will become soft and sticky, and soft candies will dry out. In other words, don't store your Crystal Candies with Southern Pralines.

Protect taffies, caramels, nougats, and popcorn balls from dampness by wrapping them individually in clear plastic wrap.

To protect brittles and toffees from dampness, layer them in an airtight container between sheets of waxed paper.

To preserve the glossy finish on chocolate-covered candies, separate chocolates from one another by storing them in paper candy cups.

To prevent divinity from quickly drying out, store it in an airtight container lined with waxed paper.

Gumdrops are an exception to storing candies tightly covered. They need to be loosely covered so their surface remains dry. Moisture makes the sugar coating soft and sticky.

Freezing candy

For longer storage, candy may be frozen. This is especially convenient when planning for the holidays.

Fudges, pralines, and caramels freeze well. Even chocolate-covered candies freeze successfully.

To freeze pan-shaped candies, remove candy from pan; place in an airtight freezer bag or container.

Chocolate-covered candy that is boxed and ready for a gift can be frozen. Just wrap the box in moisture-vaporproof wrap or place in an airtight freezer bag.

To freeze popcorn balls, first wrap the balls individually in clear plastic wrap, then place them in an airtight freezer bag.

When removing candy from the freezer, let it stand several hours to warm to room temperature before opening or removing the wrapping. This will prevent moisture from collecting on the surface of the candy and causing white speckles or gray streaks.

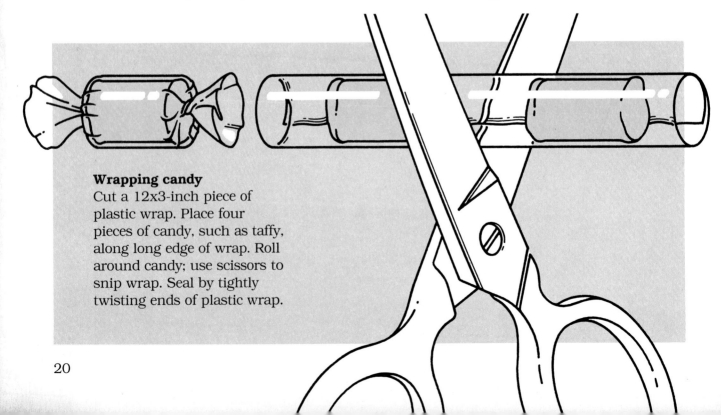

Wrapping candy

Cut a 12x3-inch piece of plastic wrap. Place four pieces of candy, such as taffy, along long edge of wrap. Roll around candy; use scissors to snip wrap. Seal by tightly twisting ends of plastic wrap.

CLASSIC CANDIES

Basic ingredients and methods for making classic candies such as Old-Time Fudge, Southern Pralines, and Basic Divinity haven't changed at all; they still require a wooden spoon and a lot of muscle for beating! But with the detailed methods and how-to photos, you won't have to rely on old-fashioned intuition. Among the other beloved candies in this chapter are Peanut Brittle, Saltwater Taffy, and Old-Fashioned Butterscotch.

Fudge and Penuche

If *one* homemade candy can be singled out as the all-time favorite, it's fudge—that creamy confection of sugar, milk, butter, and, often, chocolate.

This popular candy is said to have originated in the late nineteenth century at several women's colleges. Different fudge recipes have been found at Vassar, Wellesley, and Smith colleges.

Fudge falls into one of three categories—chocolate fudge, white or blond fudge, and penuche or brown sugar fudge. Chocolate fudge is undoubtedly the favorite, with the chocolate flavor coming from unsweetened chocolate squares, cocoa powder, or chocolate pieces. Chopped nuts are a common ingredient in this fudge. White or blond fudge features vanilla, instead of chocolate, as its basic flavor. Nuts and candied fruit are popular additions to this category. Like white or blond fudge, penuche contains no chocolate. Brown sugar, used in addition to granulated sugar, gives penuche a caramel-like flavor.

Macadamia Nut Fudge

Macadamia nuts have a flavor that resembles almonds.

1   cup coarsely chopped
    macadamia nuts
3   cups sugar
1   cup milk
2   tablespoons light corn
    syrup
3   tablespoons butter *or*
    margarine
1   teaspoon vanilla

● To toast macadamia nuts, spread nuts in a single layer in a shallow baking pan. Toast nuts in a 350° oven about 15 minutes, stirring occasionally. Reserve 2 tablespoons of the toasted nuts to sprinkle on top of the fudge.

● Line a 10x6x2-inch baking dish with foil, extending foil over edges of dish. Butter the foil; set baking dish aside.

● Butter the sides of a heavy 3-quart saucepan. In the saucepan combine the sugar, milk, and corn syrup. Cook over medium-high heat to boiling, stirring constantly with a wooden spoon to dissolve sugar. This should take about 8 minutes. Avoid splashing the mixture on sides of pan. Carefully clip the candy thermometer to side of pan.

● Cook over medium-low heat, stirring frequently, till thermometer registers 236°, soft-ball stage (see pages 10 and 11). Mixture should boil at a moderate, steady rate over the entire surface. Reaching soft-ball stage should take 25 to 35 minutes.

● Remove pan from heat. Add the 3 tablespoons butter or margarine and vanilla, but *do not stir.* Cool, without stirring, to lukewarm (110°). This should take about 55 minutes. Remove candy thermometer from saucepan.

● Beat vigorously with the wooden spoon till fudge is just beginning to thicken; add toasted nuts. Continue beating till fudge becomes very thick and just starts to lose its gloss. This should take about 8 minutes total. Quickly turn fudge into prepared dish. Sprinkle with the reserved 2 tablespoons nuts. While fudge is warm, score it into 1-inch squares. When candy is firm, use the foil to lift it out of the dish; cut candy into squares. Store tightly covered. Makes 60 pieces or about 3 pounds.

Old-Time Fudge

This is the all-time favorite classic fudge. (Pictured on page 26.)

2 cups sugar
¾ cup milk
2 squares (2 ounces)
    unsweetened chocolate,
    cut up
1 teaspoon light corn syrup
2 tablespoons butter *or*
    margarine
1 teaspoon vanilla
½ cup coarsely chopped nuts

● Line a 9x5x3-inch loaf pan with foil, extending foil over edges of pan. Butter the foil; set pan aside.

● Butter the sides of a heavy 2-quart saucepan. In the saucepan combine sugar, milk, chocolate, and corn syrup. Cook over medium-high heat to boiling, stirring constantly with a wooden spoon to dissolve sugar. This should take about 5 minutes. Avoid splashing mixture on sides of pan. Carefully clip candy thermometer to side of pan.

● Cook over medium-low heat, stirring frequently, till thermometer registers 234°, soft-ball stage (see pages 10 and 11). Mixture should boil at moderate, steady rate over entire surface. Reaching soft-ball stage should take 20 to 25 minutes.

● Remove saucepan from heat. Add the 2 tablespoons butter or margarine and vanilla, but *do not stir.* Cool, without stirring, to lukewarm (110°). This should take about 55 minutes.

● Remove the candy thermometer from the saucepan. Beat vigorously with the wooden spoon till fudge is just beginning to thicken; add nuts. Continue beating till fudge becomes very thick and just starts to lose its gloss. This should take about 7 minutes total.

● Quickly turn fudge into prepared pan. While fudge is warm, score it into 1-inch squares. When candy is firm, use foil to lift it out of the pan; cut candy into squares. (Or, to make molded shapes, lightly oil small individual candy molds or sheet candy molds. Working quickly, press fudge into molds, then unmold, using wooden picks to loosen corners. See pages 16 and 17. Allow molded fudge to set on waxed paper till firm.) Store tightly covered. Makes 45 pieces or about 1¼ pounds.

Cutting fudge into squares
While the fudge is warm, and still in the prepared 9x5x3-inch loaf pan, use a knife to mark it into 1-inch squares. (Squares are traditional, but for added interest, try cutting the fudge into diamonds or rectangles.)

When fudge is firm, use the foil to lift it out of the loaf pan. Place fudge on a cutting board, and, using a large, sharp knife, cut fudge along the markings into squares.

Opera Fudge

Even the die-hard chocolate fans on our Taste Panel found this vanilla-flavored fudge irresistible. (Pictured on page 26.)

2 cups sugar
½ cup milk
½ cup light cream
1 tablespoon light corn syrup
1 tablespoon butter *or* margarine
1 teaspoon vanilla

● Line an 8x4x2-inch loaf pan with foil, extending foil over edges of pan. Butter the foil; set pan aside.

● Butter the sides of a heavy 2-quart saucepan. In the saucepan combine sugar, milk, light cream, and corn syrup. Cook over medium-high heat to boiling, stirring constantly with a wooden spoon to dissolve sugar. This should take 5 to 7 minutes. Avoid splashing mixture on sides of pan. Carefully clip candy thermometer to side of pan.

● Cook over medium-low heat, stirring frequently, till thermometer registers 238°, soft-ball stage (see pages 10 and 11). Mixture should boil at moderate, steady rate over entire surface. Reaching soft-ball stage should take 25 to 35 minutes.

● Remove saucepan from heat. Add the 1 tablespoon butter or margarine and vanilla, but *do not stir.* Cool, without stirring, to lukewarm (110°). This should take about 55 minutes. Remove candy thermometer from saucepan. Beat vigorously with the wooden spoon till fudge becomes very thick and just starts to lose its gloss. This should take about 10 minutes.

● Quickly turn fudge into prepared pan. While fudge is warm, score it into 1-inch squares. When candy is firm, use the foil to lift it out of the pan; cut candy into squares. (Or, to make molded shapes, lightly oil small individual candy molds or candy sheet molds. Working quickly, press fudge into molds, then unmold, using toothpicks to loosen the corners. See pages 16 and 17. Allow the molded fudge to set on waxed paper till firm.) Store tightly covered. Makes 32 pieces or about 1 pound.

Almond Opera Fudge: Prepare Opera Fudge as directed above, *except* add ¼ teaspoon *almond extract* with the vanilla. Stir ⅓ cup chopped toasted *almonds* into fudge when it is just beginning to thicken. Continue beating till fudge becomes very thick and just starts to lose its gloss. This should take about 10 minutes total. Quickly turn fudge into prepared pan.

Cherry Opera Fudge: Prepare Opera Fudge as directed above, *except* stir ½ cup chopped *pecans* and ¼ cup chopped *red or green candied cherries* into fudge when it is just beginning to thicken. Continue beating till fudge becomes very thick and just starts to lose its gloss. This should take about 10 minutes total. Quickly turn fudge into prepared pan.

Mint-Layer Fudge

Topping this classic fudge with a creamy mint layer makes it even better. (Pictured on page 26.)

2 cups sugar
¾ cup milk
2 squares (2 ounces) unsweetened chocolate, cut up
1 teaspoon light corn syrup
2 tablespoons butter *or* margarine
1 teaspoon vanilla
3 tablespoons butter *or* margarine
4 teaspoons crème de menthe
1¾ cups sifted powdered sugar
½ cup chopped walnuts

● Line an 8x8x2-inch baking pan with foil, extending foil over edges of pan. Butter the foil; set pan aside.

● Butter the sides of a heavy 2-quart saucepan. In the saucepan combine sugar, milk, chocolate, and corn syrup. Cook over medium-high heat to boiling, stirring constantly with a wooden spoon to dissolve sugar. This should take about 5 minutes. Avoid splashing mixture on sides of pan. Carefully clip candy thermometer to side of pan.

● Cook over medium-low heat, stirring frequently, till thermometer registers 234°, soft-ball stage (see pages 10 and 11). Mixture should boil at a moderate, steady rate over the entire surface. Reaching soft-ball stage should take 20 to 25 minutes.

● Remove pan from heat. Add the 2 tablespoons butter or margarine and vanilla, but *do not stir.* Cool, without stirring, to lukewarm (110°). This should take about 55 minutes.

● While the fudge is cooling, prepare the mint mixture. Place the 3 tablespoons butter or margarine and the crème de menthe into a small mixer bowl. Beat with an electric mixer on high speed till fluffy. Add the powdered sugar and beat till smooth. Cover and set aside.

● Remove candy thermometer from saucepan. Beat vigorously with the wooden spoon till fudge becomes very thick and just starts to lose its gloss. This should take about 7 minutes. Quickly turn fudge into prepared pan. Dollop mint mixture over fudge; press mint mixture evenly over fudge. Sprinkle nuts over mint mixture; press in lightly. While fudge is warm, score it into 1-inch squares. When candy is firm, use the foil to lift it out of the pan; cut candy into squares. Store tightly covered. Makes 64 pieces or about 1¾ pounds.

After the fudge is turned into the prepared 8x8x2-inch baking pan, dollop the mint mixture over the fudge. Use your hands to press the mint mixture evenly over the fudge.

Sprinkle ½ cup chopped nuts over the mint mixture; press the nuts in lightly. Score the candy into 1-inch pieces while it's warm.

Honey-Walnut Penuche
(see recipe, page 32)

Old-Time Fudge
(see recipe, page 23)

Opera Fudge
(see recipe, page 24)

Mint-Layer Fudge
(see recipe, page 25)

Molasses Fudge

The combination of molasses and spices in this fudge may remind you of gingerbread.

1 cup sugar
1 cup packed brown sugar
½ cup light cream
2 tablespoons molasses
½ teaspoon ground cinnamon
¼ teaspoon ground nutmeg
⅛ teaspoon ground cloves
2 tablespoons butter *or* margarine
1½ teaspoons vanilla
½ cup coarsely chopped walnuts

● Line a 9x5x3-inch loaf pan with foil, extending foil over edges of pan. Butter the foil; set pan aside.

● Butter the sides of a heavy 2-quart saucepan. In the saucepan combine the sugar, brown sugar, cream, molasses, cinnamon, nutmeg, and cloves. Cook over medium-high heat to boiling, stirring constantly with a wooden spoon to dissolve sugars. This should take about 5 minutes. Avoid splashing mixture on sides of pan. Carefully clip candy thermometer to side of pan.

● Cook over medium-low heat, stirring frequently, till thermometer registers 240°, soft-ball stage (see pages 10 and 11). Mixture should boil at a moderate, steady rate over the entire surface. Reaching soft-ball stage should take about 12 minutes.

● Remove pan from heat. Add the 2 tablespoons butter and vanilla, but *do not stir.* Cool, without stirring, to 110°, about 55 minutes. Remove thermometer. Beat vigorously till just beginning to thicken; add nuts. Continue beating till very thick and just starts to lose its gloss. This should take about 10 minutes total. Quickly turn into prepared pan. While warm, score into 1-inch squares. When firm, lift candy out of pan; cut into squares. Store tightly covered. Makes 45 pieces or about 1 pound.

Peanut Butter Fudge

2 cups sugar
½ cup milk
⅓ cup creamy peanut butter
2 tablespoons light corn syrup
2 tablespoons butter *or* margarine
1 teaspoon vanilla
½ cup chopped peanuts

● Line an 8x8x2-inch baking pan with foil, extending foil over edges of pan. Butter the foil; set pan aside.

● Butter the sides of a heavy 2-quart saucepan. In the saucepan combine sugar, milk, peanut butter, and corn syrup. Cook over medium-high heat to boiling, stirring constantly with a wooden spoon to dissolve sugar. This should take about 5 minutes. Avoid splashing mixture on sides of pan. Carefully clip candy thermometer to side of pan.

● Cook over medium-low heat, stirring frequently, till thermometer registers 234°, soft-ball stage (see pages 10 and 11). Mixture should boil at a moderate, steady rate over the entire surface. Reaching soft-ball stage should take 8 to 10 minutes.

● Remove pan from heat. Add the 2 tablespoons butter and vanilla, but *do not stir.* Cool, without stirring, to 110°, about 55 minutes. Remove thermometer. Beat vigorously till just beginning to thicken; add nuts. Continue beating till very thick, but *still glossy.* This should take 6 to 7 minutes total. Quickly turn fudge into prepared pan. (Candy will lose its gloss after it's turned into pan.) While fudge is warm, score into 1-inch squares. When candy is firm, lift it out of pan; cut into squares. Store tightly covered. Makes 64 pieces or about 1½ pounds.

Carob Fudge

Similar in appearance to cocoa, carob powder contains its own natural sweetness, is low in fat, and is caffeine-free.

1 cup honey
1 cup creamy peanut butter
1 cup sifted unsweetened
   carob powder
1 cup chopped dried apples
   or raisins
½ cup sunflower nuts
½ cup sesame seed, toasted
½ cup crushed granola
½ cup chopped walnuts
1 tablespoon ground
   cinnamon

● Line a 9x9x2-inch baking pan with foil, extending foil over edges of pan. Butter the foil; set pan aside.
● In a heavy 3-quart saucepan combine honey and peanut butter. Cook over medium heat, stirring constantly, just till smooth. This should take about 4 minutes.
● Remove saucepan from heat. Add the carob powder, dried apples or raisins, sunflower nuts, toasted sesame seed, crushed granola, walnuts, and cinnamon; mix well. Quickly turn fudge into the prepared pan. While fudge is warm, score it into 1-inch squares. Cover and chill fudge several hours or till firm. When candy is firm, use the foil to lift it out of the pan; cut candy into squares. Store tightly covered in refrigerator. Makes 81 pieces or about 2¼ pounds.

Fudge-Making Tips

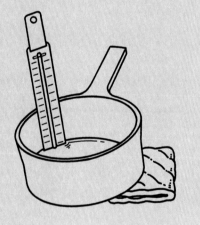

● Be sure to completely dissolve the sugar in the boiling mixture before clipping the candy thermometer to the side of the pan. You should not be able to feel sugar crystals when you rub the spoon against the side of the pan.
● To get an accurate reading when cooling fudge to 110°, the candy mixture *must* cover the bulb of the candy thermometer. If the candy mixture does not completely cover the bulb, carefully prop the saucepan with a folded hot pad so that the bulb is covered. Do this immediately after removing the pan from the heat. Then leave the pan undisturbed till the mixture cools to 110°.
● If you've beaten the fudge too long, you won't be able to turn it out of the saucepan. So instead, scrape the fudge out of the pan and knead it with your fingers; shape it into logs or roll it into 1-inch balls.

Cocoa Fudge

2 cups sugar
⅔ cup water
¼ cup unsweetened cocoa
   powder
2 tablespoons butter *or*
   margarine
1 teaspoon vanilla
½ cup chopped walnuts

● Line an 8x4x2-inch loaf pan with foil, extending foil over edges of pan. Butter the foil; set pan aside.

● Butter the sides of a heavy 2-quart saucepan. In pan combine sugar, water, and cocoa powder. Cook over medium-high heat, stirring constantly with a wooden spoon to dissolve sugar. This should take 5 to 7 minutes. Avoid splashing mixture on sides of pan. Carefully clip candy thermometer to side of pan.

● Cook over medium-low heat, stirring frequently, till thermometer registers 234°, soft-ball stage (see pages 10 and 11). Mixture should boil at a moderate, steady rate over the entire surface. Reaching soft-ball stage should take about 20 minutes.

● Remove pan from heat. Add the 2 tablespoons butter and vanilla, but *do not stir*. Cool, without stirring, to 110°, about 55 minutes. Remove thermometer. Beat vigorously till just beginning to thicken; add nuts. Continue beating till very thick and just starts to lose its gloss, about 10 minutes total. Quickly turn into prepared pan. While fudge is warm, score into 1-inch squares. When candy is firm, lift out of pan; cut into squares. Store tightly covered. Makes 32 pieces or about 1¼ pounds.

Mexican Orange Fudge

2½ cups sugar
¼ cup boiling water
½ cup light cream
2 tablespoons butter *or*
   margarine
½ cup chopped pecans
1 tablespoon finely shredded
   orange peel

● Line a 9x5x3-inch loaf pan with foil, extending foil over edges of pan. Butter the foil; set pan aside.

● To caramelize sugar, in a heavy 2-quart pan heat *1 cup* sugar over medium heat, stirring constantly, till sugar melts and turns a rich brown color. This should take 10 to 15 minutes.

● Remove pan from heat. Slowly add boiling water, stirring carefully till sugar dissolves. Add the remaining 1½ cups sugar, cream, and the 2 tablespoons butter. Cook over medium-high heat to boiling, stirring constantly to dissolve the additional sugar. This should take about 5 minutes. Avoid splashing mixture on sides of pan. Carefully clip candy thermometer to pan.

● Cook over medium-low heat, stirring frequently, till thermometer registers 240°, soft-ball stage (see pages 10 and 11). Mixture should boil at a moderate, steady rate over the entire surface. Reaching soft-ball stage should take 8 to 10 minutes.

● Remove pan from heat. Cool, without stirring, to 110°, about 55 minutes. Remove thermometer. Beat vigorously till just beginning to thicken; add pecans and orange peel. Continue beating till very thick, but *still glossy*. This should take 4 to 5 minutes total. Quickly turn fudge into prepared pan. (Candy will lose its gloss after it's turned into pan.) While warm, score into 1-inch squares. When firm, lift out of pan; cut into squares. Store tightly covered. Makes 45 pieces or about 1 pound.

Remarkable Fudge

No beating is required with this fudge!

4   cups sugar
2   5⅓-ounce cans (1⅓ cups total) evaporated milk
1   cup butter *or* margarine
1   12-ounce package (2 cups) semisweet chocolate pieces
1   7-ounce jar marshmallow creme
1   cup chopped walnuts
1   teaspoon vanilla

● Line a 13x9x2-inch baking pan with foil, extending foil over edges of pan. Butter the foil; set pan aside.

● Butter the sides of a heavy 3-quart saucepan. In the saucepan combine sugar, evaporated milk, and the 1 cup butter or margarine. Cook over medium-high heat to boiling, stirring constantly with a wooden spoon to dissolve sugar. This should take about 7 minutes. Avoid splashing mixture on sides of pan. Carefully clip candy thermometer to side of pan.

● Cook over medium heat, stirring frequently, till thermometer registers 236°, soft-ball stage (see pages 10 and 11). Mixture should boil at a moderate, steady rate over the entire surface. Reaching soft-ball stage should take 12 to 13 minutes.

● Remove saucepan from heat; remove candy thermometer from saucepan. Add chocolate pieces, marshmallow creme, chopped walnuts, and vanilla. Stir till well blended and chocolate is melted. Quickly turn fudge into prepared pan. While fudge is warm, score it into 1-inch squares. When candy is firm, use foil to lift it out of pan; cut candy into squares. Store tightly covered in refrigerator. Makes 117 pieces or about 3½ pounds.

Toasted-Coconut Fudge

Look for cream of coconut with the nonalcoholic cocktail mixes in your supermarket.

4   cups sugar
1   cup butter *or* margarine
1   5⅓-ounce can (⅔ cup) evaporated milk
½   cup cream of coconut
1   12-ounce package (2 cups) semisweet chocolate pieces
1   7-ounce jar marshmallow creme
1   teaspoon vanilla
1¼ cups coconut, toasted

● Line a 13x9x2-inch baking pan with foil, extending foil over edges of pan. Butter the foil; set pan aside.

● Butter the sides of a heavy 3-quart saucepan. In the saucepan combine sugar, the 1 cup butter or margarine, evaporated milk, and cream of coconut. Cook over medium-high heat to boiling, stirring constantly with a wooden spoon to dissolve sugar. This should take about 7 minutes. Avoid splashing mixture on sides of pan. Carefully clip candy thermometer to side of pan.

● Cook over medium-low heat, stirring frequently, till thermometer registers 236°, soft-ball stage (see pages 10 and 11). Mixture should boil at a moderate, steady rate over the entire surface. Reaching soft-ball stage should take 5 to 6 minutes.

● Remove saucepan from heat; remove candy thermometer from saucepan. Add chocolate pieces, marshmallow creme, and vanilla. Stir till well blended and chocolate is melted. Stir in *1 cup* of the toasted coconut. Quickly turn the fudge into the prepared pan. Lightly press the remaining ¼ cup toasted coconut over the top. While fudge is warm, score it into 1-inch squares. When candy is firm, use the foil to lift it out of the pan; cut candy into squares. Store tightly covered in refrigerator. Makes 117 pieces or about 3½ pounds.

Microwave Fudge

This microwave fudge is every bit as tasty as the conventional variety.

½ cup butter *or* margarine
2 cups sugar
1 5⅓-ounce can (⅔ cup) evaporated milk
2 cups tiny marshmallows
1 6-ounce package (1 cup) semisweet chocolate pieces
½ cup chopped walnuts
½ teaspoon vanilla

● Line an 8x8x2-inch baking pan with foil, extending foil over edges of pan. Butter the foil; set pan aside.

● Put the ½ cup butter or margarine into a 2½-quart nonmetal bowl. Cook, uncovered, in a countertop microwave oven on 100% power (HIGH) for 45 to 60 seconds or till the butter or margarine is melted. Add the sugar and the evaporated milk; stir till well combined. Micro-cook, uncovered, for 8 minutes, stirring every 3 minutes.

● Remove bowl from microwave oven. Add marshmallows, chocolate pieces, nuts, and vanilla. Stir till well blended and marshmallows and chocolate are melted. Quickly turn fudge into prepared pan. While fudge is warm, score it into 1-inch squares. Cool to room temperature, then chill fudge several hours or till firm. When candy is firm, use foil to lift it out of pan; cut candy into squares. Store tightly covered in refrigerator. Makes 64 pieces or about 2 pounds.

Penuche

The word penuche, usually pronounced puh-NOO-chee, comes from a Mexican-Spanish word for raw sugar. In candy-making, it refers to a fudge made with brown sugar.

1½ cups sugar
1 cup packed brown sugar
⅓ cup light cream
⅓ cup milk
2 tablespoons butter *or* margarine
1 teaspoon vanilla
½ cup chopped pecans *or* walnuts

● Line an 8x4x2-inch or a 9x5x3-inch loaf pan with foil, extending foil over edges of pan. Butter the foil; set pan aside.

● Butter the sides of a heavy 2-quart saucepan. In the saucepan combine the sugar, brown sugar, cream, and milk. Cook over medium-high heat to boiling, stirring constantly with a wooden spoon to dissolve sugars. This should take about 5 minutes. Avoid splashing mixture on sides of pan. Carefully clip candy thermometer to side of pan.

● Cook over medium-low heat, stirring frequently, till thermometer registers 236°, soft-ball stage (see pages 10 and 11). Mixture should boil at a moderate, steady rate over the entire surface. Reaching soft-ball stage should take 15 to 20 minutes.

● Remove saucepan from heat. Add the 2 tablespoons butter or margarine and vanilla, but *do not stir.* Cool, without stirring, to lukewarm (110°). This should take about 50 minutes. Remove candy thermometer from saucepan. Beat vigorously with the wooden spoon till penuche is just beginning to thicken; add nuts. Continue beating till penuche becomes very thick and just starts to lose its gloss. This should take about 10 minutes total. Quickly turn penuche into prepared pan. While penuche is warm, score it into 1-inch squares. When candy is firm, use foil to lift it out of pan; cut candy into squares. Store tightly covered. Makes about 32 pieces or about 1¼ pounds.

Coconut Penuche

1½ cups sugar
 1 cup packed brown sugar
 ⅓ cup light cream
 ⅓ cup milk
 2 tablespoons butter *or*
     margarine
 1 teaspoon vanilla
 1 3½-ounce can (1⅓ cups)
     flaked coconut

● Line an 8x4x2-inch loaf pan with foil, extending foil over edges of pan. Butter the foil; set pan aside.
● Butter the sides of a heavy 2-quart saucepan. In the saucepan combine the sugar, brown sugar, cream, and milk. Cook over medium-high heat to boiling, stirring constantly with a wooden spoon to dissolve sugars. This should take about 5 minutes. Avoid splashing mixture on sides of pan. Carefully clip candy thermometer to side of pan.
● Cook over medium-low heat, stirring frequently, till thermometer registers 236°, soft-ball stage (see pages 10 and 11). Mixture should boil at a moderate, steady rate over the entire surface. Reaching soft-ball stage should take 15 to 20 minutes.
● Remove pan from heat. Add the 2 tablespoons butter and vanilla, but *do not stir.* Cool, without stirring, to 110°, about 50 minutes. Remove thermometer. Beat vigorously till just beginning to thicken; add coconut. Continue beating till very thick and just starts to lose its gloss. This should take about 10 minutes total. Turn into prepared pan. While warm, score into 1-inch squares. When firm, lift out of pan; cut into squares. Store tightly covered. Makes 32 pieces or about 1½ pounds.

Honey-Walnut Penuche

Honey adds a smooth, satiny texture to this penuche. (Pictured on page 26.)

1½ cups sugar
 1 cup packed brown sugar
 ⅓ cup light cream
 ⅓ cup milk
 2 tablespoons honey
 2 tablespoons butter *or*
     margarine
 1 teaspoon vanilla
 ½ teaspoon finely shredded
     orange peel
 ½ cup chopped walnuts
     Walnut halves (optional)

● Line an 8x8x2-inch baking pan with foil, extending foil over edges of pan. Butter the foil; set pan aside.
● Butter the sides of a heavy 2-quart saucepan. In the saucepan combine the sugar, brown sugar, cream, milk, and honey. Cook over medium-high heat to boiling, stirring constantly with a wooden spoon to dissolve sugars. This should take about 5 minutes. Avoid splashing mixture on sides of pan. Carefully clip candy thermometer to side of pan.
● Cook over medium-low heat, stirring frequently, till thermometer registers 236°, soft-ball stage (see pages 10 and 11). Mixture should boil at a moderate, steady rate over the entire surface. Reaching soft-ball stage should take 15 to 20 minutes.
● Remove pan from heat. Add the 2 tablespoons butter, vanilla, and orange peel, but *do not stir.* Cool, without stirring, to 110°, about 50 minutes. Remove thermometer. Beat vigorously till just beginning to thicken; add nuts. Continue beating till very thick and just starts to lose its gloss. This should take about 10 minutes total. Turn into prepared pan. While warm, score into 1¼-inch squares. If desired, press a walnut half into each square. When firm, lift candy out of pan; cut into squares. Store tightly covered. Makes about 36 pieces or about 1½ pounds.

Perked-Up Penuche

The addition of coffee perks up the flavor of this penuche.

1½ cups sugar
1 cup packed brown sugar
⅓ cup light cream
⅓ cup milk
1 tablespoon instant coffee crystals
2 tablespoons butter *or* margarine
1 teaspoon vanilla
1 cup almond brickle pieces (optional)

● Line an 8x8x2-inch baking pan with foil, extending foil over edges of pan. Butter the foil; set pan aside.

● Butter the sides of a heavy 2-quart saucepan. In the saucepan combine the sugar, brown sugar, cream, milk, and coffee crystals. Cook over medium-high heat to boiling, stirring constantly with a wooden spoon to dissolve sugars. This should take about 5 minutes. Avoid splashing mixture on sides of pan. Carefully clip candy thermometer to side of pan.

● Cook over medium-low heat, stirring frequently, till thermometer registers 236°, soft-ball stage (see pages 10 and 11). Mixture should boil at a moderate, steady rate over the entire surface. Reaching soft-ball stage should take 15 to 20 minutes.

● Remove saucepan from heat. Add the 2 tablespoons butter or margarine and vanilla, but *do not stir.* Cool, without stirring, to lukewarm (110°). This should take about 50 minutes. Remove candy thermometer from saucepan. Beat vigorously with the wooden spoon till penuche is just beginning to thicken; add almond brickle pieces, if desired. Continue beating till penuche becomes very thick and just starts to lose its gloss. This should take about 10 minutes total.

● Quickly turn the penuche into the prepared pan. While penuche is warm, score it into 1-inch squares. When candy is firm, use the foil to lift it out of the pan; cut the candy into squares. Store tightly covered. Makes 64 pieces or about 1¼ pounds.

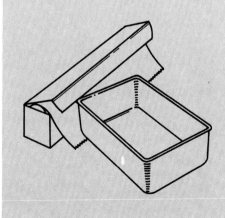

Lining Pans with Foil

Our Test Kitchen recommends lining your pans with buttered foil for two good reasons. First, grasping the pieces of foil that are extended over the edges of the pan makes it so easy to lift out the candy! And, the candy is much easier to cut when it's out of the pan. Second, you'll find the pan needs little, if any, washing when it's lined with foil.

Caramels and Pralines

Caramels and pralines are the elegant members in the family of classic candies. Both have a smooth, creamy texture and a rich, sweet flavor.

Caramels are made by boiling sugar, cream, and butter together for a long time. A few of the recipes shorten this cooking procedure by substituting sweetened condensed milk for the cream. The sweetened condensed milk has water already evaporated from it. As a result, the sugar in the milk is concentrated, causing a much shorter cooking time.

Pralines were brought to New Orleans by the early French settlers, who yearned for this favorite food. The original sugar-glazed almond recipe was adapted to the area by using native pecans and brown sugar.

Orange-Date Caramels

Sure to win compliments, these orange-flavored caramels are full of chopped dates and almonds.

1 cup sugar
1 cup whipping cream
3 tablespoons honey
2 tablespoons butter *or* margarine
1 cup chopped pitted dates
½ cup chopped almonds
1 tablespoon finely shredded orange peel

● Line an 8x4x2-inch loaf pan with foil, extending foil over edges of pan. Butter the foil; set pan aside.

● In a heavy 2-quart saucepan combine sugar, whipping cream, honey, and the 2 tablespoons butter or margarine. Cook over medium-high heat to boiling, stirring constantly with a wooden spoon to dissolve the sugar. This should take 6 to 8 minutes. Avoid splashing the mixture on sides of pan. Carefully clip candy thermometer to side of pan.

● Cook over medium heat, stirring frequently, till candy thermometer registers 250°, hard-ball stage (see pages 10 and 11). Mixture should boil at moderate, steady rate over entire surface. Reaching hard-ball stage should take about 15 minutes.

● Remove saucepan from heat; remove candy thermometer from saucepan. Immediately stir in chopped dates, chopped almonds, and finely shredded orange peel. Quickly pour the caramel mixture into prepared loaf pan.

● When caramel is firm, use foil to lift it out of pan. Use a buttered knife to cut candy into 1-inch squares. Wrap each piece in clear plastic wrap. Makes 32 pieces or about 1 pound.

Walnut Caramels

Our Taste Panel rated these creamy and chewy caramels "outstanding."(Pictured on page 37.)

1 cup chopped walnuts
1 cup butter *or* margarine
1 16-ounce package (2¼ cups packed) brown sugar
2 cups light cream
1 cup light corn syrup
1 teaspoon vanilla

● Line an 8x8x2-inch baking pan with foil, extending foil over edges of pan. Butter the foil. Sprinkle chopped walnuts on the bottom of the foil-lined pan; set pan aside.

● In a heavy 3-quart saucepan melt the 1 cup butter or margarine over low heat. Add the brown sugar, light cream, and corn syrup; mix well. Cook over medium-high heat to boiling, stirring constantly with a wooden spoon to dissolve sugar. This should take 6 to 8 minutes. Avoid splashing the mixture on sides of pan. Carefully clip candy thermometer to side of pan.

● Cook over medium heat, stirring frequently, till candy thermometer registers 248°, firm-ball stage (see pages 10 and 11). Mixture should boil at moderate, steady rate over entire surface. Reaching firm-ball stage should take 45 to 55 minutes.

● Remove saucepan from heat; remove candy thermometer from saucepan. Immediately stir in vanilla. Quickly pour the caramel mixture over the nuts in the prepared pan.

● When caramel is firm, use foil to lift it out of pan. Use a buttered knife to cut candy into 1-inch squares. Wrap each piece in clear plastic wrap. Makes 64 pieces or about 2 pounds.

Boiling the caramel mixture
When clipping the candy thermometer to the side of the saucepan, make sure the bulb is completely covered with boiling liquid and that it doesn't touch the bottom of the saucepan. This ensures a more accurate temperature reading.

The caramel mixture should boil at a moderate, steady rate over the entire surface. Stir frequently till mixture reaches 248°.

Shortcut Caramels

Substituting sweetened condensed milk for cream cuts the cooking time in half.

1 cup butter *or* margarine
1 16-ounce package (2¼ cups packed) brown sugar
1 14-ounce can (1¼ cups) *sweetened condensed milk*
1 cup light corn syrup
1 teaspoon vanilla

● Line a 9x9x2-inch baking pan with foil, extending foil over edges of pan. Butter the foil; set pan aside.
● In a heavy 3-quart saucepan melt the 1 cup butter or margarine over low heat. Add brown sugar, sweetened condensed milk, and light corn syrup; mix well. Carefully clip candy thermometer to side of pan.
● Cook over medium heat, stirring frequently, till thermometer registers 248°, firm-ball stage (see pages 10 and 11). Mixture should boil at a moderate, steady rate over the entire surface. Reaching firm-ball stage should take 15 to 20 minutes.
● Remove saucepan from heat; remove candy thermometer from saucepan. Immediately stir in vanilla. Quickly pour the caramel mixture into prepared baking pan. When caramel is firm, use foil to lift it out of pan. Use a buttered knife to cut candy into 1-inch squares. Wrap each piece in clear plastic wrap. Makes 81 pieces or about 2¾ pounds.

Chocolate Shortcut Caramels: Prepare Shortcut Caramels as directed above, *except* melt 2 squares (2 ounces) *unsweetened chocolate* with the butter or margarine.

Mocha Caramels

Mocha is the smooth, rich flavor that results from blending chocolate and coffee together.

½ cup butter *or* margarine
2 squares (2 ounces) unsweetened chocolate
2 cups sugar
1 cup packed brown sugar
1 cup light cream
1 cup light corn syrup
2 tablespoons instant coffee crystals

● Line a 9x9x2-inch baking pan with foil, extending foil over edges of pan. Butter the foil; set pan aside.
● In a heavy 3-quart saucepan melt the ½ cup butter or margarine and unsweetened chocolate over low heat. Add sugar, brown sugar, cream, corn syrup, and coffee crystals; mix well. Cook over medium-high heat to boiling, stirring constantly with a wooden spoon to dissolve sugars. This should take 6 to 8 minutes. Avoid splashing mixture on sides of pan. Carefully clip candy thermometer to side of pan.
● Cook over medium heat, stirring frequently, till thermometer registers 248°, firm-ball stage (see pages 10 and 11). Mixture should boil at a moderate, steady rate over the entire surface. Reaching firm-ball stage should take 45 to 55 minutes.
● Remove saucepan from heat; remove candy thermometer from saucepan. Quickly pour the caramel mixture into the prepared pan. When caramel is firm, use the foil to lift it out of the pan. Use a buttered knife to cut the candy into 1-inch squares. Wrap each piece in clear plastic wrap. Makes 81 pieces or about 2¼ pounds.

Walnut Caramels
(see recipe, page 35)

Chocolate Pralines
(see recipe, page 40)

Buttermilk Pralines
(see recipe, page 39)

Marbled Caramels

Swirling chocolate caramel into vanilla caramel gives a marbled effect.

1 cup butter *or* margarine
1 16-ounce package (2¼ cups packed) brown sugar
2 cups light cream
1 cup light corn syrup
1 teaspoon vanilla
1 square (1 ounce) unsweetened chocolate, melted and cooled

● Line a 9x9x2-inch baking pan with foil, extending foil over edges of pan. Butter the foil; set pan aside.

● In a heavy 3-quart saucepan melt the 1 cup butter or margarine over low heat. Add brown sugar, cream, and corn syrup; mix well. Cook over medium-high heat to boiling, stirring constantly with a wooden spoon to dissolve sugar. This should take 6 to 8 minutes. Avoid splashing mixture on sides of pan. Carefully clip candy thermometer to side of pan.

● Cook over medium heat, stirring frequently, till candy thermometer registers 248°, firm-ball stage (see pages 10 and 11). Mixture should boil at a moderate, steady rate over the entire surface. Reaching firm-ball stage should take 45 to 55 minutes.

● Remove saucepan from heat; remove candy thermometer from saucepan. Immediately stir in the vanilla. Quickly pour *slightly more than half* of the caramel mixture into the prepared pan. Stir the melted and cooled chocolate into the remaining caramel mixture in the saucepan. Pour chocolate mixture over the caramel mixture in the baking pan. *Gently* zigzag a narrow metal spatula through mixtures to swirl.

● When caramel is firm, use foil to lift it out of the pan. Use a buttered knife to cut candy into 1-inch squares. Wrap each piece in clear plastic wrap. Makes 81 pieces or about 2 pounds.

Marbling the caramel mixtures

After pouring the chocolate caramel mixture over the vanilla caramel mixture in the prepared baking pan, use a narrow metal spatula to *gently* zigzag through the mixtures. Do not zigzag too vigorously or the marble effect will be lost.

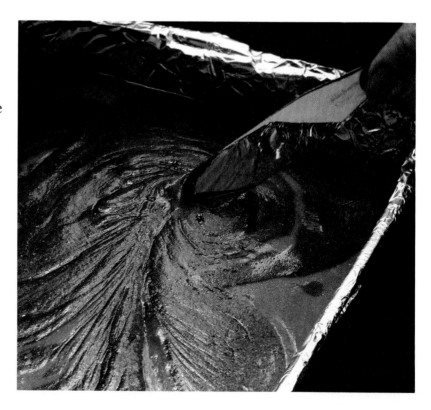

Buttermilk Pralines

Don't substitute sour milk for the buttermilk in this recipe. (Pictured on page 37.)

2 cups packed dark brown
   sugar
1 cup buttermilk
2 tablespoons butter *or*
   margarine
2 cups broken *or* chopped
   pecans

● Butter the sides of a heavy 2-quart saucepan. In the saucepan combine brown sugar and buttermilk. Cook over medium-high heat to boiling, stirring constantly with a wooden spoon to dissolve sugar. This should take 6 to 8 minutes. Avoid splashing mixture on sides of pan. Carefully clip candy thermometer to pan. Cook over medium-low heat, stirring occasionally, till thermometer registers 234°, soft-ball stage (see pages 10 and 11). Mixture should boil at a moderate, steady rate over entire surface. Reaching soft-ball stage should take 20 to 25 minutes.
● Remove saucepan from heat. Add the 2 tablespoons butter or margarine, but *do not stir*. Cool, without stirring, to 150°. This should take about 30 minutes. Remove candy thermometer from saucepan. Immediately stir in pecans. Beat vigorously with the wooden spoon till candy is just beginning to thicken, but is still glossy. This should take 3 to 4 minutes.
● Quickly drop the candy from a teaspoon onto a baking sheet lined with waxed paper. If the candy becomes too stiff to drop easily from the spoon, stir in a few drops of *hot water*. Store tightly covered. Makes about 36 pralines.

Brown Sugar Pralines: Prepare Buttermilk Pralines as directed above, *except* substitute 1 cup *light cream* for buttermilk.

Maple-Walnut Pralines

2 cups packed brown sugar
1 cup light cream
2 tablespoons butter *or*
   margarine
1 cup coarsely chopped
   walnuts
1 teaspoon maple flavoring

● Butter the sides of a heavy 2-quart saucepan. In the saucepan combine brown sugar and cream. Cook over medium-high heat to boiling, stirring constantly with a wooden spoon to dissolve sugar. This should take 6 to 8 minutes. Avoid splashing mixture on sides of pan. Carefully clip candy thermometer to side of pan. Cook over medium-low heat, stirring occasionally, till thermometer registers 234°, soft-ball stage (see pages 10 and 11). Mixture should boil at a moderate, steady rate over the entire surface. Reaching soft-ball stage should take 20 to 25 minutes.
● Remove saucepan from heat. Add the 2 tablespoons butter or margarine, but *do not stir*. Cool, without stirring, to 150°. This should take about 30 minutes. Remove candy thermometer from pan. Immediately stir in nuts and maple flavoring. Beat vigorously with the wooden spoon till candy is just beginning to thicken, but is still glossy. This should take 3 to 4 minutes.
● Quickly drop the candy from a teaspoon onto a baking sheet lined with waxed paper. If the candy becomes too stiff to drop easily from the spoon, stir in a few drops of *hot water*. Store tightly covered. Makes about 24 pralines.

Southern Pralines

In Dixie, where pralines originated, they're traditionally made with pecans. (Chocolate Pralines are pictured on page 37.)

1½ cups sugar
1½ cups packed brown sugar
 1 cup light cream
 3 tablespoons butter *or* margarine
 2 cups pecan halves

● Butter the sides of a heavy 2-quart saucepan. In the saucepan combine sugar, brown sugar, and cream. Cook over medium-high heat to boiling, stirring constantly with a wooden spoon to dissolve sugars. This should take 6 to 8 minutes. Avoid splashing mixture on sides of pan. Carefully clip candy thermometer to pan. Cook over medium-low heat, stirring occasionally, till thermometer registers 234°, soft-ball stage (see pages 10 and 11). Mixture should boil at moderate, steady rate over entire surface. Reaching soft-ball stage should take 16 to 18 minutes.
● Remove pan from heat. Add the 3 tablespoons butter, but *do not stir*. Cool, without stirring, to 150°, about 30 minutes. Remove thermometer. Immediately stir in pecans. Beat vigorously with the wooden spoon till candy is just beginning to thicken but is still glossy. This should take 2 to 3 minutes.
● Drop from a teaspoon onto a baking sheet lined with waxed paper. If candy becomes too stiff to drop, stir in a few drops of *hot water*. Store tightly covered. Makes about 36 pralines.

Chocolate Pralines: Prepare Southern Pralines as directed above, *except* add 2 squares (2 ounces) cut-up *unsweetened chocolate* with the butter or margarine.

1 After the praline mixture has cooled to 150°, immediately stir in the nuts. Beat vigorously with the wooden spoon till the mixture is just beginning to thicken, but is still glossy.

2 Drop the candy from a teaspoon onto waxed paper. Work quickly so candy does not set up in the pan. If the candy becomes too stiff to drop easily, stir in a few drops of *hot water*.

Black Walnut Pralines

For slightly firmer pralines, wait a day before serving them.

1½ cups sugar
1½ cups packed brown sugar
  1 cup light cream
  3 tablespoons butter *or*
      margarine
  1 cup broken black walnuts
  1 cup raisins
  1 teaspoon vanilla

● Butter the sides of a heavy 2-quart saucepan. In the saucepan combine sugar, brown sugar, and light cream. Cook over medium-high heat to boiling, stirring constantly with a wooden spoon to dissolve sugars. This should take 6 to 8 minutes. Avoid splashing mixture on sides of pan. Carefully clip candy thermometer to side of saucepan.

● Cook over medium-low heat, stirring occasionally, till thermometer registers 234°, soft-ball stage (see pages 10 and 11). Mixture should boil at a moderate, steady rate over entire surface. Reaching soft-ball stage should take 16 to 18 minutes.

● Remove saucepan from heat. Add the 3 tablespoons butter or margarine, but *do not stir*. Cool, without stirring, to 150°. This should take about 30 minutes. Remove thermometer from pan. Immediately stir in walnuts, raisins, and vanilla. Beat vigorously with the wooden spoon till mixture is just beginning to thicken but is still glossy. This should take about 3 minutes.

● Quickly drop the candy from a teaspoon onto a baking sheet lined with waxed paper. If the candy becomes too stiff to drop easily from the spoon, stir in a few drops of *hot water*. Makes about 36 pralines.

Peanut Patties

Similar to pralines, this candy is made with powdered sugar.

  2 cups sugar
  1 5⅓-ounce can (⅔ cup)
      evaporated milk
  ½ cup light corn syrup
  1 cup sifted powdered sugar
  2 teaspoons vanilla
1½ cups dry roasted peanuts

● Butter the sides of a heavy 2-quart saucepan. In the saucepan combine sugar, evaporated milk, and light corn syrup. Cook over medium-high heat to boiling, stirring constantly with a wooden spoon to dissolve sugar. This should take about 4 minutes. Avoid splashing mixture on sides of saucepan. Carefully clip candy thermometer to side of saucepan.

● Cook over medium-low heat, stirring occasionally, till thermometer registers 234°, soft-ball stage (see pages 10 and 11). Mixture should boil at a moderate, steady rate over the entire surface. Reaching soft-ball stage should take about 20 minutes.

● Remove saucepan from heat. Cool, without stirring, to 150°. This should take about 30 minutes. Remove candy thermometer from saucepan. Immediately stir in the powdered sugar and vanilla. Add the dry roasted peanuts. Beat vigorously with the wooden spoon till candy is just beginning to thicken but is still glossy. This should take 1 to 2 minutes.

● Quickly drop the candy from a teaspoon onto a baking sheet lined with waxed paper. If the candy becomes too stiff to drop easily from the spoon, stir in a few drops of *hot water*. Store tightly covered. Makes about 36 patties.

Divinity and Nougat

Many of the classic candies found in this book are closely related, but divinity and nougat are truly first cousins.

Although divinity has a light, soft texture, and nougat has a dense, chewy texture, these candies are related because they use several similar ingredients and require beating a sugar syrup into beaten egg whites.

In the past, the vigorous beating that's required for successful divinity or nougat caused many cooks to shy away from making either candy. Today, however, with the help of sturdy, freestanding electric mixers, these two favorite candies can be whipped up with relative ease.

Basic Divinity

First master the basic divinity, then try the pinwheel variation. (Pinwheel Divinity is pictured on page 44.)

2½ cups sugar
½ cup light corn syrup
½ cup water
2 egg whites
1 teaspoon vanilla
1 *or* 2 drops desired food
coloring (optional)
½ cup chopped nuts
(optional)

● In a heavy 2-quart saucepan combine sugar, light corn syrup, and water. Cook over medium-high heat to boiling, stirring constantly with a wooden spoon to dissolve sugar. This should take 5 to 7 minutes. Avoid splashing mixture on sides of pan. Carefully clip candy thermometer to side of pan.

● Cook over medium heat, without stirring, till thermometer registers 260°, hard-ball stage (see pages 10 and 11). Mixture should boil at a moderate, steady rate over the entire surface. Reaching hard-ball stage should take about 15 minutes.

● Remove saucepan from heat; remove thermometer from saucepan. In a large mixer bowl, immediately beat egg whites with a sturdy, freestanding electric mixer on medium speed till stiff peaks form (tips stand straight).

● *Gradually* pour hot mixture in a thin stream (slightly less than ⅛-inch diameter) over egg whites, beating with the electric mixer on high speed and scraping the sides of the bowl occasionally. This should take about 3 minutes. (Add mixture *slowly* to ensure proper blending.)

● Add vanilla and food coloring, if desired. Continue beating with the electric mixer on high speed, scraping the sides of the bowl occasionally, just till candy starts to lose its gloss. When beaters are lifted, mixture should fall in a ribbon, but mound on itself and not disappear into remaining mixture. Final beating should take 5 to 6 minutes.

● Drop a spoonful of the mixture onto waxed paper. If it stays mounded in a soft shape, it is beaten properly. Immediately stir in nuts, if desired. Quickly drop the remaining mixture from a teaspoon onto a baking sheet lined with waxed paper. If mixture flattens, beat ½ to 1 minute more; check again. If mixture is stiff to spoon and has a rough surface, beat in *hot water*, a few drops at a time, till it is a softer consistency. Store tightly covered. Makes about 40 pieces.

Pinwheel Divinity: Lightly sprinkle two pastry cloths or waxed paper with sifted *powdered sugar.*

Prepare Basic Divinity as directed on opposite page, *except* substitute ½ teaspoon *peppermint extract* for the vanilla and omit the nuts.

When candy holds its shape, turn *half* of the mixture onto the dusted pastry cloth or the waxed paper. Quickly roll candy into a 13-inch square. Tint the remaining candy with a few drops of *red food coloring.* Roll out remaining candy as directed above.

Invert one of the divinity squares over the other; press the squares together lightly. Quickly roll up jelly-roll style; press to seal edge. Cut the roll into ⅜-inch slices. Makes about 34 slices.

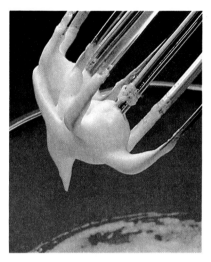

1 As soon as sugar mixture reaches 260°, begin beating egg whites with a sturdy, freestanding electric mixer. Beat till stiff peaks form (tips stand straight when beaters are lifted).

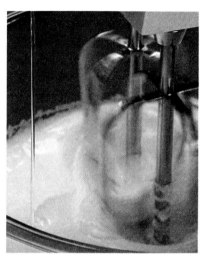

2 *Gradually* pour the hot mixture in a thin stream (slightly less than ⅛-inch diameter) over egg whites, beating with the electric mixer on high speed. Scrape sides of bowl occasionally.

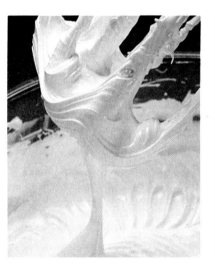

3 Continue beating just till the candy starts to lose its gloss. When beaters are lifted, mixture should fall in a ribbon, but mound on itself and not disappear into the remaining mixture.

4 Once the candy is beaten properly, work quickly so it does not get stiff. Use a second spoon to push the candy off the first one. If the candy does become too stiff to spoon, beat in a few drops of *hot water.*

Black Walnut Nougat
(see recipe, page 48)

Chocolate Mint Divinity

Pinwheel Divinity
(see recipe, page 43)

Chocolate Mint Divinity

2 8-ounce bars milk chocolate
2½ cups sugar
½ cup light corn syrup
½ cup water
2 egg whites
2 squares (2 ounces)
    unsweetened chocolate,
    melted and cooled
½ teaspoon peppermint
    extract
¼ cup crushed
    peppermint candies

● Line a 9x9x2-inch baking pan with foil, extending foil over edges of pan. Butter foil; line with chocolate bars. Set pan aside.
● In a heavy 2-quart saucepan combine sugar, corn syrup, and water. Cook over medium-high heat to boiling, stirring constantly with a wooden spoon to dissolve sugar. This should take 5 to 7 minutes. Avoid splashing mixture on sides of pan. Carefully clip candy thermometer to pan. Cook over medium heat, without stirring, to 260°, hard-ball stage (see pages 10 and 11). Mixture should boil at moderate, steady rate over entire surface. Reaching hard-ball stage should take about 15 minutes.
● Remove pan from heat; remove thermometer. In a large mixer bowl, immediately beat egg whites with a sturdy, freestanding electric mixer till stiff peaks form (tips stand straight).
● *Gradually* pour hot mixture in a thin stream (slightly less than ⅛-inch diameter) over egg whites, beating on high speed and scraping bowl occasionally. This should take about 3 minutes. (Add mixture *slowly* to ensure proper blending.) Add unsweetened chocolate and peppermint extract. Continue beating on high speed, scraping bowl occasionally, just till candy starts to lose its gloss. When beaters are lifted, mixture should fall in a ribbon, but mound on itself and not disappear into remaining mixture. Final beating should take 5 to 6 minutes.
● Immediately spread over chocolate bars in prepared pan. Sprinkle with crushed candies. When firm, lift out of pan; cut into 1-inch squares. Store tightly covered. Makes 81 pieces.

Tips for Making Divinity and Nougat

● Use a sturdy, freestanding electric mixer when making these two candies. Both require heavy beating, which puts a strain on mixer motors. Portable mixers and some lightweight, freestanding mixers don't have the power necessary for this chore.
● Plan to make these candies on a relatively dry day. Because sugar absorbs humidity, no amount of beating on a humid day will make these candies set up.
● Allow the egg whites to come to room temperature before beating. That way, they'll whip up to their maximum volume.
● Never double divinity or nougat recipes. The mixture will not cook properly and will be too much for your mixer to handle.

Maple-Orange Divinity Cutouts

2½ cups sugar
 ½ cup light corn syrup
 ½ cup water
 2 egg whites
 1 teaspoon finely shredded
    orange peel
 1 teaspoon maple flavoring
    Finely chopped nuts
    (optional)

● Line a 9x9x2-inch baking pan with foil, extending foil over edges of pan. Butter the foil; set pan aside.

● In a heavy 2-quart saucepan combine sugar, corn syrup, and water. Cook over medium-high heat to boiling, stirring constantly with a wooden spoon to dissolve sugar. This should take 5 to 7 minutes. Avoid splashing mixture on sides of pan. Carefully clip candy thermometer to side of pan. Cook over medium heat, without stirring, till thermometer registers 260°, hard-ball stage (see pages 10 and 11). Mixture should boil at a moderate, steady rate over the entire surface. Reaching hard-ball stage should take about 15 minutes.

● Remove pan from heat; remove thermometer. In a large mixer bowl, immediately beat egg whites with a sturdy, freestanding electric mixer till stiff peaks form (tips stand straight).

● *Gradually* pour hot mixture in a thin stream (slightly less than ⅛-inch diameter) over egg whites, beating on high speed and scraping bowl occasionally. This should take about 3 minutes. (Add mixture *slowly* to ensure proper blending.)

● Add the orange peel and maple flavoring. Continue beating on high speed, scraping bowl occasionally, just till candy starts to lose its gloss. When beaters are lifted, mixture should fall in a ribbon, but mound on itself and not disappear into remaining mixture. Final beating should take 5 to 6 minutes.

● Immediately spread candy into the prepared pan. When candy is firm, use foil to lift it out of the pan. Lightly oil 1½-inch cookie cutters and cut candy into desired shapes. Cut shapes as close together as possible. If desired, roll cut edges in finely chopped nuts. Store tightly covered. Makes about 25 pieces.

Cutting out divinity shapes
Line a 9x9x2-inch baking pan with foil; butter the foil. When the candy mounds on itself, quickly spread it into the prepared pan. Once the candy is firm, use the foil to lift it out of the pan.

Lightly oil 1½-inch cookie cutters and cut candy into desired shapes. Cut the shapes as close together as possible so very little candy is left over. If desired, roll cut edges of the candy in finely chopped nuts.

Spumoni Divinity

Working quickly is a must when making this layered candy.

2½ cups sugar
½ cup light corn syrup
½ cup water
2 egg whites
½ teaspoon rum flavoring
¼ cup finely chopped red candied cherries
¼ cup finely chopped pistachios *or* almonds
3 *or* 4 drops green food coloring

● Line a 10x6x2-inch baking dish with foil, extending foil over edges of dish. Butter the foil; set dish aside.

● In a heavy 2-quart saucepan combine sugar, light corn syrup, and water. Cook over medium-high heat to boiling, stirring constantly with a wooden spoon to dissolve sugar. This should take 5 to 7 minutes. Avoid splashing mixture on sides of pan. Carefully clip candy thermometer to side of pan.

● Cook over medium heat, without stirring, till thermometer registers 260°, hard-ball stage (see pages 10 and 11). The mixture should boil at moderate, steady rate over entire surface. Reaching hard-ball stage should take about 15 minutes.

● Remove saucepan from heat; remove candy thermometer from saucepan. In a large mixer bowl, immediately begin to beat egg whites with a sturdy, freestanding electric mixer on medium speed till stiff peaks form (tips stand straight).

● *Gradually* pour hot mixture in a thin stream (slightly less than ⅛-inch diameter) over egg whites, beating with the electric mixer on high speed and scraping sides of bowl occasionally. This should take about 3 minutes. (Add mixture *slowly* to ensure proper blending.)

● Add rum flavoring. Continue beating with electric mixer on high speed, scraping sides of bowl occasionally, just till candy starts to lose its gloss. When beaters are lifted, mixture should fall in a ribbon, but mound on itself and not disappear into remaining mixture. Final beating should take 5 to 6 minutes.

● Immediately spread *one-third* of the candy into the prepared dish. Sprinkle with the chopped candied cherries. Quickly stir finely chopped pistachios or almonds and food coloring into the remaining candy. Immediately spread over cherry layer in baking dish. When candy is firm, use foil to lift it out of dish; cut into 1-inch squares. Store tightly covered. Makes 60 pieces.

Basic Nougat

Preparing nougat is similar to making divinity, but nougat is cooked to a higher temperature, so the candy has a chewier texture. (Black Walnut Nougat is pictured on page 44.)

Cornstarch
1½ cups sugar
1 tablespoon cornstarch
1 cup light corn syrup
½ cup water
2 egg whites
1 teaspoon vanilla
1 cup slivered almonds, toasted

● Line a 9x9x2-inch baking pan with foil, extending foil over edges of pan. Butter the foil; sprinkle with a small amount of cornstarch. Set pan aside.

● In a heavy 2-quart saucepan combine sugar and the 1 table-spoon cornstarch. Add the light corn syrup and water; mix well. Cook over medium-high heat to boiling, stirring constantly with a wooden spoon to dissolve sugar. This should take 5 to 7 minutes. Avoid splashing mixture on sides of pan. Carefully clip candy thermometer to side of pan.

● Cook over medium heat, stirring occasionally, till thermometer registers 286°, soft-crack stage (see pages 10 and 11). Mixture should boil at a moderate, steady rate over entire surface. Reaching soft-crack stage should take 20 to 25 minutes.

● Remove saucepan from heat; remove candy thermometer from saucepan. In a large mixer bowl, immediately beat egg whites with a sturdy, freestanding electric mixer on medium speed till stiff peaks form (tips stand straight).

● *Gradually* pour hot mixture in a thin stream (slightly less than ⅛-inch diameter) over egg whites, beating with the electric mixer on high speed and scraping the sides of the bowl occasionally. This should take about 3 minutes. (Add mixture *slowly* to ensure proper blending.)

● Add vanilla. Continue beating with the electric mixer on high speed, scraping the sides of the bowl occasionally, till candy becomes very thick and less glossy. When beaters are lifted, mixture should fall in a ribbon, but mound on itself, then slowly disappear into the remaining mixture. Final beating should take 5 to 6 minutes.

● Immediately stir in toasted almonds. Quickly turn nougat mixture into the prepared pan. While nougat is warm, score it into about 2x¾-inch pieces. When candy is firm, use foil to lift it out of pan; cut candy into pieces. Wrap each piece in clear plastic wrap. Store tightly covered. Makes about 48 pieces.

Black Walnut Nougat: Prepare Basic Nougat as directed above, *except* substitute ½ cup chopped *black walnuts* for the almonds. While nougat is warm, score it into about 1½x1¼-inch pieces. When candy is firm, use foil to lift it out of pan; cut candy into pieces. Garnish top of each piece with a drained and halved *maraschino cherry*. Makes about 42 pieces.

Mocha Nougat

A subtle combination of cocoa and coffee flavors this nougat.

Cornstarch
1½ cups sugar
3 tablespoons unsweetened
   cocoa powder
1 tablespoon cornstarch
1½ teaspoons instant coffee
   crystals
1 cup light corn syrup
½ cup water
2 egg whites
½ cup slivered almonds,
   toasted

● Line a 9x9x2-inch baking pan with foil, extending foil over edges of pan. Butter the foil; sprinkle with a small amount of cornstarch. Set pan aside.

● In a heavy 3-quart saucepan combine sugar, cocoa powder, the 1 tablespoon cornstarch, and coffee crystals. Add corn syrup and water; mix well. Cook over medium-high heat to boiling, stirring constantly with a wooden spoon to dissolve sugar. This should take 5 to 7 minutes. Avoid splashing mixture on sides of pan. Carefully clip candy thermometer to side of pan.

● Cook over medium heat, stirring occasionally, till thermometer registers 286°, soft-crack stage (see pages 10 and 11). Mixture should boil at a moderate, steady rate over the entire surface. Reaching soft-crack stage should take about 20 to 25 minutes.

● Remove saucepan from heat; remove candy thermometer from saucepan. In a large mixer bowl, immediately beat egg whites with a sturdy, freestanding electric mixer on medium speed till stiff peaks form (tips stand straight).

● *Gradually* pour hot mixture in a thin stream (slightly less than ⅛-inch diameter) over the egg whites, beating with the electric mixer on high speed and scraping the sides of the bowl occasionally. This should take about 3 minutes. (Add mixture *slowly* to ensure proper blending.)

● Continue beating with the electric mixer on high speed, scraping the sides of the bowl occasionally, till candy becomes very thick and less glossy. When beaters are lifted, mixture should fall in a ribbon, but mound on itself, then slowly disappear into the remaining mixture. Final beating should take 5 to 6 minutes.

● Immediately stir in almonds. Quickly turn nougat mixture into the prepared pan. While nougat is warm, score it into about 2x¾-inch pieces. When candy is firm, use foil to lift it out of the pan; cut candy into pieces. Wrap each piece in clear plastic wrap. Store tightly covered. Makes about 48 pieces.

Taffy, Creams, and Fondant

Taffy and fondant are either pulled or kneaded to develop their smooth textures. Creams, on the other hand, get their velvety texture from rich ingredients.

Because it takes *a lot* of pulling to make taffy, why not have an old-fashioned taffy pull? Guests of all ages will have almost as much fun pulling this candy as they will have eating it.

Unlike taffy, which is pulled to its correct texture, fondant is kneaded for a soft, smooth texture. Fondant comes from a French word meaning "to melt." Use this rich, smooth, melt-in-your-mouth candy as the basis for mint patties, or roll it into small balls and dip it into melted chocolate.

You also can stuff dried dates or figs with this versatile candy. The number of uses for fondant is limited only by the cook's imagination.

Like fondant, creams are rolled into small balls and dipped into melted chocolate. Or, for an equally delightful flavor, simply coat the creams with powdered sugar or finely chopped nuts.

Maple Taffy

This taffy mixture fills a 1½-quart saucepan, so watch it carefully as it cooks.

1 cup maple-flavored syrup
¾ cup sugar
¾ cup light corn syrup
½ cup water
2 tablespoons butter *or* margarine

● Butter a 15x10x1-inch baking pan; set pan aside. Butter the sides of a heavy 1½-quart saucepan. In the saucepan combine maple-flavored syrup, sugar, corn syrup, and water. Cook over medium heat to boiling, stirring constantly with a wooden spoon to dissolve sugar. This should take about 7 minutes. Avoid splashing mixture on sides of pan. Carefully clip candy thermometer to side of pan.
● Cook over medium-low heat, without stirring, till the thermometer registers 265°, hard-ball stage (see pages 10 and 11). Mixture should boil at a moderate, steady rate over the entire surface. Reaching hard-ball stage should take 35 to 40 minutes.
● Remove saucepan from heat; remove candy thermometer from saucepan. Stir in the 2 tablespoons butter or margarine. Pour the mixture into prepared baking pan. Cool till taffy mixture can be handled easily. This should take about 15 minutes.
● Butter hands; twist and pull candy till it turns a creamy color and is stiff and quite difficult to pull. This should take about 10 minutes. Candy is ready to snip if it cracks when tapped on work surface (see page 14).
● Divide the candy into fourths; twist and pull each piece into a long strand about ½ inch thick. With buttered scissors, snip each strand of taffy into bite-size pieces. Wrap each piece in clear plastic wrap. Makes about 1¼ pounds.

Saltwater Taffy
(see recipe, page 52)

Fancy Liqueur Chocolates
(see recipe, page 83)

Saltwater Taffy

Originating at New Jersey seashore resorts, this candy gets its name from its oceanside origin. (Pictured on page 51.)

2 cups sugar
1 cup light corn syrup
1 cup water
1½ teaspoons salt
2 tablespoons butter *or* margarine
¼ teaspoon peppermint extract *or* rum flavoring, *or* few drops oil of cinnamon (optional)
Few drops red food coloring (optional)

● Butter a 15x10x1-inch baking pan; set pan aside. Butter the sides of a heavy 2-quart saucepan. In the saucepan combine sugar, light corn syrup, water, and salt. Cook over medium-high heat to boiling, stirring constantly with a wooden spoon to dissolve sugar. This should take about 10 minutes. Avoid splashing mixture on sides of pan. Carefully clip candy thermometer to side of pan.

● Cook over medium heat, without stirring, till thermometer registers 265°, hard-ball stage (see pages 10 and 11). Mixture should boil at a moderate, steady rate over the entire surface. Reaching hard-ball stage should take about 40 minutes.

● Remove saucepan from heat; remove candy thermometer from saucepan. Stir in the 2 tablespoons butter or margarine. Stir in peppermint extract, rum flavoring, or oil of cinnamon and food coloring, if desired. Pour the mixture into the prepared baking pan. Cool till taffy mixture can be handled easily. This should take 15 to 20 minutes.

● Butter hands; twist and pull candy till it turns a creamy color and is stiff and quite difficult to pull. This should take about 10 minutes. Candy is ready to snip if it cracks when tapped on work surface (see page 14).

● Divide the candy into fourths; twist and pull each piece into a long strand about ½ inch thick. With buttered scissors, snip each strand of taffy into bite-size pieces. Wrap each piece in clear plastic wrap. Makes about 1½ pounds.

Cutting and storing taffy
After dividing the candy into fourths, twist and pull each piece into long strands about ½ inch thick. Using buttered scissors, snip each strand of the taffy into bite-size pieces.

To prevent the taffy from becoming soft and sticky during storage, wrap each piece in clear plastic wrap.

Old-Fashioned Molasses Taffy

2   cups sugar
1   cup molasses
½   cup water
½   cup butter *or* margarine
¼   cup light corn syrup

● Butter a 15x10x1-inch baking pan; set aside. Butter sides of a heavy 3-quart saucepan. In pan combine sugar, molasses, water, the ½ cup butter, and corn syrup. Cook over medium heat to boiling, stirring constantly with a wooden spoon to dissolve sugar. This should take about 5 minutes. Avoid splashing mixture on sides of pan. Carefully clip candy thermometer to pan.
● Cook over medium-low heat, without stirring, till thermometer registers 265°, hard-ball stage (see pages 10 and 11). Mixture should boil at a moderate, steady rate over entire surface. Reaching hard-ball stage should take about 40 minutes.
● Remove pan from heat; remove thermometer. Pour into prepared pan. Cool till mixture can be handled easily. This should take 15 to 20 minutes. Butter hands; twist and pull candy till it turns a creamy color and is stiff and quite difficult to pull. This should take about 10 minutes. Candy is ready to snip if it cracks when tapped on work surface (see page 14). Divide candy into fourths; twist and pull each piece into a long strand about ½ inch thick. With buttered scissors, snip into bite-size pieces. Wrap each piece in clear plastic wrap. Makes about 1½ pounds.

Coconut-Pineapple Creams

2   cups sugar
½   cup water
¼   cup light cream
1   tablespoon light corn syrup
⅓   cup coconut
⅓   cup finely chopped candied
      pineapple
1   pound dipping chocolate *or*
      confectioner's coating

● Butter the sides of a heavy 2-quart saucepan. In pan combine sugar, water, cream, and corn syrup. Cook over medium-high heat to boiling, stirring constantly with a wooden spoon to dissolve sugar. This should take 5 to 6 minutes. Avoid splashing mixture on sides of pan. Carefully clip candy thermometer to pan. Cook over medium-low heat, stirring occasionally, till thermometer registers 240°, soft-ball stage (see pages 10 and 11). Mixture should boil at a moderate, steady rate over entire surface. Reaching soft-ball stage should take 15 to 20 minutes.
● Remove pan from heat. Cool, without stirring, to 110°. This should take about 45 minutes. Remove thermometer. Beat with the wooden spoon till candy is just beginning to thicken; add coconut and pineapple. Continue beating till creamy and slightly stiff. This should take about 5 minutes total.
● Shape candy into 1-inch balls; place on waxed paper. Let stand about 20 minutes or till dry. Melt dipping chocolate or confectioner's coating (see dipping instructions on pages 18 and 19). Dip balls into the melted chocolate. Let stand till dry. Store tightly covered in a cool, dry place. Makes about 40 pieces.

Note: If desired, immediately after shaping the candy into 1-inch balls, roll the balls in sifted *powdered sugar* or finely chopped *nuts* instead of dipping them into melted chocolate.

Cherry Creams

2 **cups sugar**
½ **cup water**
¼ **cup light cream**
1 **tablespoon light corn syrup**
¼ **cup finely chopped candied cherries**
Few drops cherry flavoring
1 **pound dipping chocolate** *or* **confectioner's coating**

● Butter the sides of a heavy 2-quart saucepan. In pan combine sugar, water, cream, and corn syrup. Cook over medium-high heat to boiling, stirring constantly with a wooden spoon to dissolve sugar. This should take 5 to 6 minutes. Avoid splashing mixture on sides of pan. Carefully clip candy thermometer to pan. Cook over medium-low heat, stirring occasionally, till thermometer registers 240°, soft-ball stage (see pages 10 and 11). Mixture should boil at a moderate, steady rate over entire surface. Reaching soft-ball stage should take 15 to 20 minutes.
● Remove pan from heat. Cool, without stirring, to 110°. This should take about 45 minutes. Remove thermometer. Beat with wooden spoon till candy is just beginning to thicken; add candied cherries and cherry flavoring. Continue beating till creamy and slightly stiff. This should take about 5 minutes total.
● Shape candy into 1-inch balls; place balls on waxed paper. Let stand about 20 minutes or till dry. Melt dipping chocolate or confectioner's coating (see dipping instructions on pages 18 and 19). Dip balls into the melted chocolate. Let stand till dry. Store tightly covered in a cool, dry place. Makes about 40 pieces.

Note: If desired, immediately after shaping the candy into 1-inch balls, roll the balls in sifted *powdered sugar* or finely chopped *nuts* instead of dipping them into melted chocolate.

Chocolate Buttercreams

½ **cup light corn syrup**
⅓ **cup butter** *or* **margarine**
1 **square (1 ounce) unsweetened chocolate, cut up**
1 **teaspoon vanilla**
4 **cups sifted powdered sugar**
1 **pound dipping chocolate** *or* **confectioner's coating**

● Butter a baking sheet; set baking sheet aside. In a heavy 3-quart saucepan combine light corn syrup, the ⅓ cup butter or margarine, and unsweetened chocolate. Cook over medium heat to boiling, stirring constantly with a wooden spoon. This should take 8 to 9 minutes.
● Remove saucepan from heat; add vanilla. Stir in the powdered sugar, *1 cup* at a time, till well combined. Turn candy mixture onto the prepared baking sheet. Cool till the mixture can be handled easily. This should take about 15 minutes. Knead mixture about 5 minutes or till smooth.
● Shape candy into 1-inch balls; place balls on waxed paper. Let stand about 20 minutes or till dry. Melt dipping chocolate or confectioner's coating (see dipping instructions on pages 18 and 19). Dip balls into the melted chocolate. Let stand till dry. Store tightly covered in a cool, dry place. Makes about 60 pieces.

Note: If desired, immediately after shaping the candy into 1-inch balls, roll the balls in sifted *powdered sugar* or finely chopped *nuts* instead of dipping them into melted chocolate.

Peanut Butter Balls

These creamy peanut butter centers don't require any cooking.

1 cup sifted powdered sugar
½ cup creamy peanut butter
3 tablespoons butter *or* margarine, softened
1 pound dipping chocolate *or* confectioner's coating

● In a mixing bowl stir together powdered sugar, creamy peanut butter, and butter or margarine till well combined.
● Shape candy into 1-inch balls; place the balls on a baking sheet lined with waxed paper. Let the balls stand about 20 minutes or till dry.
● Melt the dipping chocolate or confectioner's coating (see dipping instructions on pages 18 and 19). Dip the peanut butter balls into the melted chocolate. Let stand till dry. Store tightly covered in a cool, dry place. Makes about 30 pieces.

Note: If desired, immediately after shaping the candy into 1-inch balls, roll the balls in sifted *powdered sugar* or finely chopped *peanuts* instead of dipping them into melted chocolate.

Chocolate Truffles

Dropping the chocolate mixture from a teaspoon causes the typical irregular shape of this candy.

6 squares (6 ounces) semisweet chocolate, coarsely chopped
¼ cup butter *or* margarine
3 tablespoons whipping cream
1 beaten egg yolk
3 tablespoons desired liquor* *or* whipping cream
1 pound dipping chocolate *or* confectioner's coating

● In a heavy 2-quart saucepan combine semisweet chocolate, butter or margarine, and 3 tablespoons whipping cream. Cook over low heat, stirring constantly, till chocolate is melted. This should take about 10 minutes.
● Remove saucepan from heat. Gradually stir about *half* of the hot mixture into the beaten egg yolk. Return egg mixture to saucepan. Cook over medium heat, stirring constantly, till slightly thickened. This should take about 2 minutes.
● Remove saucepan from heat. Stir in desired liquor or 3 tablespoons whipping cream. Transfer chocolate mixture to a small mixer bowl. Chill about 1 hour or till mixture is completely cool and smooth, stirring occasionally.
● Beat the cooled chocolate mixture with an electric mixer on medium speed till slightly fluffy. This should take about 2 minutes. Chill about 15 minutes or till mixture holds its shape. Drop mixture from a level teaspoon onto a baking sheet lined with waxed paper. Chill about 30 minutes more or till firm.
● Melt dipping chocolate (see dipping instructions on pages 18 and 19). Dip candy into the melted chocolate. Let stand till dry. Store tightly covered in a cool, dry place. Makes about 48 pieces.

Note: If desired, after chilling the shaped candy for 30 minutes, roll it in *unsweetened cocoa powder* or finely chopped *nuts* instead of dipping it into melted chocolate.

*Use rum, Irish whiskey, or brandy.

Fondant

To get a smooth, creamy fondant, let the candy stand (ripen) for 24 hours.

2 cups sugar
1½ cups water
2 tablespoons light corn
    syrup *or* ⅛ teaspoon
    cream of tartar

● Butter the sides of a heavy 1½-quart saucepan. In pan combine sugar, water, and corn syrup. Cook over medium-high heat to boiling, stirring constantly with a wooden spoon to dissolve sugar. This should take 6 to 8 minutes. Avoid splashing mixture on sides of pan. Cover and cook about 45 seconds more. Uncover; carefully clip candy thermometer to side of pan.
● Cook over medium-low heat, without stirring, till thermometer registers 240°, soft-ball stage (see pages 10 and 11). Mixture should boil at a moderate, steady rate over the entire surface. Reaching soft-ball stage should take about 35 minutes.
● Remove pan from heat; remove thermometer. Pour mixture onto a large platter. *Do not scrape pan.* Cool, without stirring, till slightly warm to the touch. This should take about 50 minutes. Beat with the wooden spoon till candy is white and firm. This should take about 10 minutes. Knead 5 minutes or till smooth. Form into a ball; wrap in clear plastic wrap. Let ripen at room temperature for 24 hours. Use to make Mint Patties, to dip into chocolate, or to stuff dried fruit. Makes about ¾ pound.

Mint Patties: Prepare Fondant as above. In top of a double boiler heat and stir ripened fondant over hot, not boiling, water just till melted and smooth. Remove pan from heat, leaving fondant over hot water. Stir in 1 tablespoon softened *butter or margarine,* a few drops *oil of peppermint,* and a few drops *food coloring,* if desired. Drop from a teaspoon onto baking sheet lined with waxed paper, swirling tops. Makes about 36 patties.

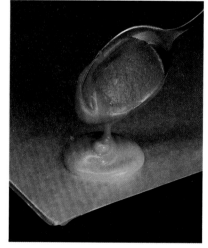

1 Drop the melted fondant onto a baking sheet lined with waxed paper.

2 Lift teaspoon off the patty in a circular motion, making a swirl on the top.

Brittle, Toffee, and Hard Candy

Some of the oldest, most popular gift-giving candies are brittles, toffees, and hard candies. What better way to say, "You're special," than to give someone a gift from your kitchen.

Brittles are probably the oldest of the three candies. Although peanut brittle is most common, brittle made with other kinds of nuts is equally tasty. Stretching this candy into a thin sheet makes it brittle.

Toffees are kissing cousins to brittles, but have a rich, buttery flavor because a large amount of butter is added. It's important to use only butter to make toffees. When margarine is used, the fat separates out onto the surface of the candy.

A jar of old-fashioned hard candies adds sparkle to any occasion. The bite-size candies not only glitter with color, but they also are loaded with flavor.

Orange-Coconut Brittle

Placing waxed paper between the layers of brittle during storage will prevent the candy from sticking together. (Pictured on page 60.)

2 cups sugar
1 cup light corn syrup
1 teaspoon finely shredded orange peel
½ cup orange juice
2 tablespoons butter *or* margarine
1½ teaspoons baking soda, sifted
1 cup coconut

● Butter two large baking sheets; set baking sheets aside. Butter the sides of a heavy 3-quart saucepan. In the saucepan combine sugar, light corn syrup, shredded orange peel, orange juice, and the 2 tablespoons butter or margarine. Cook over medium-high heat to boiling, stirring constantly with a wooden spoon to dissolve sugar. This should take about 5 minutes. Avoid splashing mixture on sides of saucepan. Carefully clip the candy thermometer to side of saucepan.

● Cook over medium-low heat, stirring frequently, till thermometer registers 295°, hard-crack stage (see pages 10 and 11). Mixture should boil at a moderate, steady rate over entire surface. Reaching hard-crack stage should take about 25 minutes.

● Remove saucepan from heat; remove candy thermometer from saucepan. Quickly sprinkle the sifted baking soda over the mixture, stirring constantly. Immediately pour mixture onto prepared baking sheets; sprinkle with coconut.

● If desired, stretch the candy by using two forks to lift and pull the candy as it cools. Pull gently to avoid tearing the candy. Cool completely. Break candy into pieces. Store tightly covered. Makes about 1½ pounds.

Buttery Cashew Brittle

2 cups sugar
1 cup light corn syrup
1 cup butter
½ cup water
3 cups cashews,
    coarsely chopped
1½ teaspoons baking soda,
    sifted

● Butter two large baking sheets; set baking sheets aside. Butter the sides of a heavy 3-quart saucepan. In the saucepan combine sugar, corn syrup, the 1 cup butter, and water. Cook over medium-high heat to boiling, stirring constantly with a wooden spoon to dissolve sugar. This should take about 8 minutes. Avoid splashing mixture on sides of pan. Carefully clip candy thermometer to side of pan.

● Cook over medium heat, stirring occasionally, till thermometer registers 275°, soft-crack stage (see pages 10 and 11). Mixture should boil at a moderate, steady rate over the entire surface. Reaching soft-crack stage should take 20 to 25 minutes. Stir in the chopped cashews. Continue cooking over medium heat, stirring frequently, till thermometer registers 295°, hard-crack stage. Reaching hard-crack stage should take about 7 to 10 minutes more.

● Remove pan from heat; remove thermometer. Quickly sprinkle sifted baking soda over mixture, stirring constantly. Immediately pour mixture onto prepared baking sheets. If desired, stretch candy by using two forks to lift and pull candy as it cools. Pull gently to avoid tearing. Cool completely. Break candy into pieces. Store tightly covered. Makes about 2¼ pounds.

Peanut Brittle

This popular brittle is loaded with nuts. (Pictured on page 60.)

2 cups sugar
1 cup light corn syrup
½ cup water
¼ cup butter *or* margarine
2½ cups raw peanuts
1½ teaspoons baking soda,
    sifted

● Butter two large baking sheets; set baking sheets aside. Butter the sides of a heavy 3-quart saucepan. In the saucepan combine sugar, corn syrup, water, and the ¼ cup butter or margarine. Cook over medium-high heat to boiling, stirring constantly with a wooden spoon to dissolve sugar. This should take about 5 minutes. Avoid splashing mixture on sides of pan. Carefully clip candy thermometer to side of pan.

● Cook over medium-low heat, stirring occasionally, till thermometer registers 275°, soft-crack stage (see pages 10 and 11). Mixture should boil at a moderate, steady rate over entire surface. Reaching soft-crack stage should take 30 to 35 minutes. Stir in nuts. Continue cooking over medium-low heat, stirring frequently, till thermometer registers 295°, hard-crack stage. Reaching hard-crack stage should take 15 to 20 minutes more.

● Remove pan from heat; remove thermometer. Quickly sprinkle sifted baking soda over mixture, stirring constantly. Immediately pour mixture onto prepared baking sheets. If desired, stretch candy by using two forks to lift and pull candy as it cools. Pull gently to avoid tearing. Cool completely. Break candy into pieces. Store tightly covered. Makes about 2⅓ pounds.

1 Mixing soda into the candy mixture

As soon as the candy thermometer registers 295° (hard-crack stage), remove the saucepan from the heat. Remove the candy thermometer from the saucepan.

Stir constantly as you sprinkle the sifted baking soda over the candy mixture. The candy will foam as the baking soda reacts chemically to neutralize the acid of the caramelized sugar. This makes the brittle porous and tender.

2 Stretching the brittle into a thin sheet

As the candy cools on the buttered baking sheet, stretch it into a thin sheet by lifting and pulling the candy with two forks. Try to pull the candy gently to avoid tearing it. Stretching the brittle into a thin sheet will help make it crisp.

When candy is completely cooled, break it into pieces. An easy way to do this is to crack it with the handle of a wooden spoon or with the back of a heavy knife.

Orange-Coconut Brittle
(see recipe, page 57)

Peanut Brittle
(see recipe, page 58)

Crystal Candies
(see recipe, page 64)

Caramelized Peanut Brittle

Caramelized sugar gives this brittle its rich, distinctive flavor.

1 **tablespoon butter** *or*
  margarine
1 **cup chopped peanuts**
2 **cups sugar**

● Butter a large baking sheet; set the baking sheet aside. In a small saucepan melt the 1 tablespoon butter or margarine over low heat. Stir in the chopped peanuts; keep the peanuts warm over low heat.

● To caramelize the sugar, in a heavy 10-inch skillet heat sugar over medium heat, stirring constantly, till sugar melts and turns a rich brown color. This should take 12 to 15 minutes.

● Remove the skillet from the heat; quickly stir in the warm chopped peanuts. Immediately pour the mixture onto the prepared baking sheet.

● If desired, stretch the candy by using two forks to lift and pull the candy as it cools. Pull gently to avoid tearing the candy. Cool completely. Break the candy into pieces. Store tightly covered. Makes about 1¼ pounds.

Caramelizing sugar
Caramelizing sugar actually means melting sugar. As the sugar melts, it becomes a rich brown liquid.

To caramelize the sugar, place it in a heavy 10-inch skillet. Heat the sugar over medium heat, stirring with a wooden spatula or spoon, till the sugar melts and turns a rich brown color. Make sure to stir the sugar constantly so it doesn't scorch.

Toffee Butter Crunch

Because of the large amount of butter in it, toffee won't stick to the unbuttered foil.

½ cup coarsely chopped
   pecans *or* toasted
   almonds
1 cup butter
1 cup sugar
3 tablespoons water
1 tablespoon light corn syrup
¾ cup semisweet *or* milk
   chocolate pieces
½ cup finely chopped pecans
   or toasted almonds

● Line a 13x9x2-inch baking pan with foil, extending foil over edges of pan. Sprinkle the ½ cup coarsely chopped nuts on bottom of foil-lined pan; set pan aside. Butter the sides of a heavy 2-quart saucepan. In pan melt the 1 cup butter over low heat. Stir in sugar, water, and corn syrup. Cook over medium-high heat to boiling, stirring constantly with a wooden spoon to dissolve sugar. This should take about 4 minutes. Avoid splashing mixture on sides of pan. Clip candy thermometer to pan.

● Cook over medium heat, stirring frequently, till thermometer registers 290°, soft-crack stage (see pages 10 and 11). Mixture should boil at a moderate, steady rate over the entire surface. Reaching soft-crack stage should take about 15 minutes. Watch carefully after candy mixture reaches 280°.

● Remove pan from heat; remove thermometer. Pour mixture into prepared pan. Let stand 2 to 3 minutes or till surface is firm. Sprinkle with chocolate pieces; let stand 1 to 2 minutes. When softened, spread pieces evenly over mixture. Sprinkle with the ½ cup finely chopped nuts; press nuts lightly into melted chocolate. Chill till firm. Lift candy out of pan; break into pieces. Store tightly covered. Makes about 1½ pounds.

Peanut Butter Toffee

Peanuts and peanut butter-flavored topping give this toffee its peanutty-good flavor.

½ cup coarsely chopped
   peanuts
1 cup butter
1 cup sugar
3 tablespoons water
1 tablespoon light corn syrup
1 6-ounce package (1 cup)
   peanut butter-flavored
   pieces
½ cup finely chopped peanuts

● Line a 13x9x2-inch baking pan with foil, extending foil over edges of pan. Sprinkle the ½ cup coarsely chopped peanuts on bottom of foil-lined pan; set pan aside. Butter sides of a heavy 2-quart saucepan. In pan melt the 1 cup butter over low heat. Stir in sugar, water, and corn syrup. Cook over medium-high heat to boiling, stirring constantly with a wooden spoon to dissolve sugar. This should take about 4 minutes. Avoid splashing mixture on sides of pan. Carefully clip candy thermometer to pan.

● Cook over medium heat, stirring frequently, till thermometer registers 290°, soft-crack stage (see pages 10 and 11). Mixture should boil at a moderate, steady rate over the entire surface. Reaching soft-crack stage should take about 15 minutes. Watch carefully after candy mixture reaches 280°.

● Remove pan from heat; remove thermometer. Pour mixture into prepared pan. Let stand 2 to 3 minutes or till surface is firm. Sprinkle with peanut butter-flavored pieces; let stand 1 to 2 minutes. When softened, spread pieces evenly over mixture. Sprinkle with ½ cup finely chopped peanuts; press nuts lightly into melted pieces. Chill till firm. Lift candy out of pan; break into pieces. Store tightly covered. Makes about 1½ pounds.

Brown Sugar Toffee

Using butter instead of margarine when making toffees will keep the fat from separating out onto the surface of the candy.

½ cup coarsely chopped
    walnuts
1 cup butter
1¼ cups packed brown sugar
3 tablespoons water
1 tablespoon light corn syrup
½ cup finely chopped walnuts

● Line a 13x9x2-inch baking pan with foil, extending foil over edges of pan. Sprinkle the ½ cup coarsely chopped walnuts on bottom of foil-lined pan; set pan aside.

● Butter the sides of a heavy 2-quart saucepan. In the saucepan melt the 1 cup butter over low heat. Stir in brown sugar, water, and corn syrup. Cook over medium-high heat to boiling, stirring constantly with a wooden spoon to dissolve sugar. This should take about 4 minutes. Avoid splashing mixture on sides of pan. Carefully clip candy thermometer to side of pan.

● Cook over medium heat, stirring frequently, till thermometer registers 290°, soft-crack stage (see pages 10 and 11). Mixture should boil at a moderate, steady rate over the entire surface. Reaching soft-crack stage should take about 15 minutes. Watch carefully after candy mixture reaches 280°.

● Remove pan from heat; remove thermometer. Pour mixture into the prepared pan. Sprinkle with the ½ cup finely chopped walnuts. When firm, lift candy out of pan; break candy into pieces. Store tightly covered. Makes about 1¼ pounds.

Double Chocolate-Almond Toffee

½ cup slivered almonds,
    toasted
1 cup butter
1 cup sugar
3 tablespoons water
1 tablespoon light corn syrup
1 square (1 ounce)
    unsweetened chocolate,
    melted and cooled
¾ cup semisweet chocolate
    pieces

● Line a 13x9x2-inch baking pan with foil, extending foil over edges of pan. Sprinkle the toasted almonds on the bottom of foil-lined pan; set pan aside.

● Butter the sides of a heavy 2-quart saucepan. In pan melt the 1 cup butter over low heat. Stir in sugar, water, and corn syrup. Cook over medium-high heat to boiling, stirring constantly with a wooden spoon to dissolve sugar. This should take about 4 minutes. Carefully clip candy thermometer to side of pan.

● Cook over medium heat, stirring frequently, till thermometer registers 230°, thread stage (see pages 10 and 11). Mixture should boil at a moderate, steady rate over the entire surface. Reaching thread stage should take 4 to 5 minutes. Stir in the unsweetened chocolate. Continue cooking over medium heat, stirring frequently, till thermometer registers 290°, soft-crack stage. Reaching soft-crack stage should take about 15 minutes more. Watch carefully after candy mixture reaches 280°.

● Remove pan from heat; remove thermometer. Pour mixture into the prepared pan. Let stand 2 to 3 minutes or till surface is firm. Sprinkle with chocolate pieces; let stand 1 to 2 minutes. When softened, spread pieces evenly over mixture. Chill till firm. Lift candy out of pan; break candy into pieces. Store tightly covered. Makes about 1⅓ pounds.

Crystal Candies

Make different shapes by using candy molds. (Pictured on page 60.)

2 cups sugar
1 cup light corn syrup
½ cup water
¼ teaspoon desired food
   coloring
   Few drops oil of cinnamon,
      oil of peppermint, *or*
      oil of wintergreen

● Line an 8x8x2-inch baking pan with foil, extending foil over edges of pan. Butter the foil; set pan aside.
● Butter the sides of a heavy 2-quart saucepan. In saucepan combine sugar, corn syrup, and water. Cook over medium-high heat to boiling, stirring constantly with a wooden spoon to dissolve sugar. This should take about 5 minutes. Avoid splashing mixture on sides of pan. Carefully clip candy thermometer to side of saucepan.
● Cook over medium heat, stirring occasionally, till thermometer registers 290°, soft-crack stage (see pages 10 and 11). Mixture should boil at a moderate, steady rate over the entire surface. Reaching soft-crack stage should take 20 to 25 minutes. Remove the saucepan from heat; remove candy thermometer from the saucepan.
● Quickly stir in desired food coloring and flavoring. Immediately pour mixture into the prepared pan. Let stand 5 to 10 minutes or till a film forms over the surface of the candy.
● Using a broad spatula or pancake turner, begin marking candy by pressing a line across surface, ½ inch from edge of pan. Do not break film on surface. Repeat along other three sides of pan, intersecting lines at corners to form squares. (If candy does not hold its shape, it is not cool enough to mark. Let candy stand a few more minutes and start again.)
● Continue marking lines along all sides, ½ inch apart, till you reach center. Retrace previous lines, pressing the spatula deeper but not breaking film on surface. Repeat till the spatula can be pressed to bottom of pan along all lines. Cool completely. Use foil to lift the candy out of the pan; break candy into squares.
● (Or, to make molded candies, oil molds made for hard candies. Pour mixture into molds. Cool 10 minutes or till firm. Invert; twist molds till candies come out. Cool completely; decorate candies with Powdered Sugar Icing, if desired.) Store tightly covered. Makes about 1½ pounds.

Powdered Sugar Icing: Combine 1 cup sifted *powdered sugar*, ¼ teaspoon *vanilla*, and enough *milk* (about 4 teaspoons) to make of spreading consistency.

Old-Fashioned Butterscotch

These little pieces of candy are packed with a rich, buttery flavor.

1 cup sugar
¼ cup light corn syrup
2 tablespoons water
1½ teaspoons vinegar
¼ cup butter *or* margarine, cut into 8 pieces
¼ teaspoon vanilla

● Line an 8x8x2-inch baking pan with foil, extending foil over edges of pan. Butter the foil; set pan aside.

● Butter the sides of a heavy 1-quart saucepan. In the saucepan combine sugar, light corn syrup, water, and vinegar. Cook over medium-high heat to boiling, stirring constantly with a wooden spoon to dissolve sugar. This should take about 5 minutes. Avoid splashing mixture on sides of pan. Carefully clip candy thermometer to side of pan.

● Cook over medium heat, stirring constantly, while adding the ¼ cup butter or margarine, two pieces at a time. Continue cooking over medium heat, stirring occasionally, till thermometer registers 300°, hard-crack stage (see pages 10 and 11). Mixture should boil at a moderate, steady rate over the entire surface. Reaching hard-crack stage should take 25 to 30 minutes.

● Remove saucepan from heat; remove thermometer from saucepan. Stir in vanilla. Pour mixture into prepared pan. Let stand 5 to 10 minutes or till a film forms over surface of candy.

● Using a broad spatula or pancake turner, begin marking candy by pressing a line across surface, ½ inch from edge of pan. Do not break the film on the surface. Repeat along other three sides of pan, intersecting lines at corners to form squares. (If candy does not hold its shape, it is not cool enough to mark. Let candy stand a few more minutes and start again.)

● Continue marking lines along all sides, ½ inch apart, till you reach the center. Retrace previous lines, pressing the spatula deeper but not breaking film on surface. Repeat till the spatula can be pressed to bottom of pan along all lines.

● Cool completely. Use the foil to lift candy out of the pan; break into squares. Store tightly covered. Makes about ⅔ pound.

Cleaning Candy-Making Equipment

To clean cooking utensils easily, place them in the dirty saucepan and fill the saucepan with *hot* water. Bring the water to boiling; simmer till the hardened candy is dissolved. Then wash the saucepan and utensils in hot, soapy water. Rinse and dry thoroughly.

SPECIALTY CANDIES

For an extra-special treat, try your hand at making gumdrops, candy bars, and marshmallows. You'll discover they're even better when they're homemade!

Dipped cream centers, Chocolate-Covered Cherries, Caramel Corn, sugared and spiced nuts, and fruit confections are also here. We have included them in this chapter because we think they're very special, too!

Fruit and Nut Confections

Fruits and nuts of all sorts make simple, yet sophisticated, confections.

Goodies prepared with combinations of dried fruits are limitless. The natural sweetness and bright colors of the fruits are a welcome addition to any candy tray.

Sugared and glazed nuts traditionally are associated with weddings and teas. The keeping qualities of these nut confections add to their popularity. If they're kept refrigerated or frozen, the nuts retain their freshness for several weeks.

Microwave Apricot Balls

Taste the tang of the apricots and enjoy the crunch of the shredded wheat cereal with every bite of this nutritious candy!

⅓ cup butter *or* margarine
1 slightly beaten egg
1 cup snipped dried apricots
¾ cup sugar
¼ cup all-purpose flour
2 cups bite-size shredded wheat squares, coarsely crushed
½ cup chopped walnuts
¼ teaspoon almond extract

● Place the butter or margarine in a 2½-quart nonmetal bowl. Cook, uncovered, in a countertop microwave oven on 100% power (HIGH) for 30 seconds to 1 minute or till melted. Add the slightly beaten egg, snipped dried apricots, sugar, and flour; stir till well combined.

● Micro-cook, uncovered, for 3½ to 4½ minutes or till very thick, stirring every minute. Remove bowl from microwave oven. Cool the apricot mixture about 5 minutes.

● Add the crushed shredded wheat squares, the chopped walnuts, and the almond extract to the apricot mixture; stir till well combined.

● Shape the apricot mixture into 1-inch balls. Store tightly covered in refrigerator. Makes about 40 pieces.

Candied Fruit Peel

Nibble on these delicious candied peels, or use them in recipes calling for candied orange peel.

3 medium oranges *or*
   tangelos, *or* 8
   medium tangerines
Cold water
2 cups sugar
½ cup water
Sugar

● Using the point of a sharp knife, cut the peels of the oranges, tangelos, or tangerines into quarters. Using the bowl of a spoon, loosen the peel from the pulp and membrane of the fruit, leaving the white pith attached to the peel. (Save the pulp of the fruit for another use.)

● Place the fruit peel in a 2½-quart nonmetal bowl. Add enough cold water to the bowl to cover the fruit peel. Weight the peel down with a plate, if necessary, to keep the peel under the water. Let the fruit peel stand overnight weighted down in the cold water.

● Drain the fruit peel; rinse it thoroughly in cold water. Place the fruit peel in a 2-quart saucepan. Cover the fruit peel with fresh cold water and heat to boiling. Remove saucepan from heat; let stand 10 minutes. Drain fruit peel. Repeat the boiling and standing process three more times. (This helps remove the bitter taste from the peel.) After draining the fruit peel for the last time, let it stand till thoroughly cooled.

● With kitchen scissors, cut the cooled fruit peel into strips about ¼ inch wide. In a saucepan combine the 2 cups sugar and the ½ cup water. Cook over medium-high heat to boiling, stirring constantly with a wooden spoon to dissolve sugar. This should take 5 to 7 minutes. Carefully add the fruit peel strips to the saucepan.

● Cook over medium-low heat, stirring occasionally, till fruit peel is translucent and most of the liquid is absorbed. Mixture should boil at a moderate, steady rate over the entire surface. This should take 25 to 30 minutes.

● Drain the fruit peel thoroughly; cool to lukewarm. While peel is still slightly sticky, roll it in the additional sugar to coat. Place coated fruit peel on a wire rack for 1 to 2 hours or till dry. Store tightly covered. Makes about 4 cups.

1 Removing the peel

Using the point of a sharp knife, cut the peels of the oranges, tangelos, or tangerines into quarters. With the bowl of a spoon, loosen the peel from the pulp and membrane of the fruit, leaving the white pith attached to the peel.

An elegant touch

Make your candied fruit peels even more of a delicacy by dipping them into chocolate! After drying the candied peels thoroughly, hold a peel by one end and dip it into melted chocolate. (Or, to completely cover the peel, drop it into the chocolate and use a fork to remove it.)

Place the dipped peels on waxed paper and let them stand till the chocolate is dry.

2 Rolling the peel in sugar

Cook the fruit peel till it's transparent and most of the liquid in the saucepan has been absorbed. Drain the peel thoroughly. When the peel is lukewarm, but still slightly sticky, roll it in sugar. Place the peel on a wire rack to dry completely.

No-Cook Fruit Balls

For a tropical taste treat, try these easy-to-make fruit balls. (Pictured on page 72.)

¾ cup pitted dried prunes
¾ cup pitted whole dates
½ cup dried apricots
½ cup blanched whole
      almonds
¼ cup raisins
 2 tablespoons frozen orange
      juice concentrate
 2 teaspoons honey *or*
      molasses
1¼ cups coconut

● Using a food processor or a food grinder with a coarse blade, grind together the dried prunes, whole dates, dried apricots, blanched whole almonds, and raisins. Turn ground mixture into a mixing bowl. Add the frozen orange juice concentrate and the honey or molasses; stir till well combined.
● Shape mixture into 1-inch balls. Roll the balls in coconut. Store tightly covered in refrigerator. Makes about 36 pieces.

Swedish Nuts

The meringue coating gives the nuts a slightly foamy but crisp coating.

 3 cups walnut *or* pecan halves
 2 egg whites
      Dash salt
¾ cup sugar
½ cup butter *or* margarine

● To toast the walnut or pecan halves, spread the nuts in a single layer in a shallow baking pan. Toast nuts in a 350° oven about 10 minutes, stirring occasionally.
● To make the meringue, in a large mixer bowl beat egg whites and salt with an electric mixer on medium speed till soft peaks form (tips curl). Gradually add the sugar, about 1 tablespoon at a time, beating with the electric mixer on high speed and scraping the sides of the bowl occasionally. Continue beating with the electric mixer on high speed, scraping the sides of the bowl occasionally till stiff peaks form (tips stand straight). Fold the toasted walnut or pecan halves into the meringue.
● Melt the butter or margarine in a 15x10x1-inch baking pan. Spread the meringue mixture over the melted butter or margarine. Bake in a 325° oven about 30 minutes or till the meringue mixture is a light golden brown color and all the butter or margarine is absorbed. During baking, stir the meringue mixture about every 8 minutes. Cool completely. Store tightly covered. Makes about 2 pounds.

Caramel Pecan Logs

Caramel and chopped nuts surround a creamy, smooth fondant center.

Fondant, ripened
(see recipe, page 56)
1 14-ounce package vanilla
   caramels
3 tablespoons butter *or*
   margarine
2 tablespoons milk
2 cups chopped pecans *or*
   peanuts

● Prepare Fondant according to recipe directions. Let stand (ripen) at room temperature for 24 hours.
● Divide ripened fondant into fourths. Shape each piece into a 3-inch-long log. In a heavy 1½-quart saucepan combine caramels, butter or margarine, and milk. Cook over low heat, stirring occasionally, till caramels are melted. Meanwhile, spread chopped pecans or peanuts on a piece of waxed paper.
● Remove the saucepan from heat. Carefully dip the fondant logs, one at a time, into the melted caramel mixture. Use a fork to turn the log in the caramel mixture to coat it on all sides. Lift the log out of the caramel mixture with the fork. Let excess caramel drip off the log.
● Place the dipped log on the chopped pecans or peanuts. Use the waxed paper to roll the dipped log in the chopped nuts till it is covered. Place logs on a baking sheet lined with waxed paper. Chill about 1 hour or till firm. To serve, let logs stand at room temperature about 30 minutes; cut into ¼-inch slices. Makes about 48 slices.

**Rolling logs
in chopped nuts**
Spread the chopped pecans or peanuts on a piece of waxed paper. After dipping a fondant log into the melted caramel mixture, place it on the chopped nuts. Use the waxed paper to help you roll the log in the nuts till it's well coated.

   After rolling each log in nuts, place it on a baking sheet lined with waxed paper. Refrigerate about 1 hour or till firm. Before serving, let the logs stand at room temperature about 30 minutes. This will make the logs easier to slice. Cut logs into ¼-inch-thick slices.

No-Cook Fruit Balls
(see recipe, page 70)

Orange Gumdrops
(see recipe, page 76)

Glazed Almonds

Coffee Walnuts

Glazed Almonds

These glossy, coated nuts have a rich, buttery flavor.

2 cups blanched whole
   almonds
½ cup sugar
2 tablespoons butter *or*
   margarine
½ teaspoon vanilla

● Line a baking sheet with foil. Butter the foil; set baking sheet aside.

● In a heavy 10-inch skillet combine the almonds, sugar, and the 2 tablespoons butter or margarine. Cook over medium heat, stirring constantly, till the sugar melts and turns a rich brown color. This should take about 9 minutes.

● Remove skillet from heat. Immediately stir in the vanilla. Spread almond mixture onto the prepared baking sheet. Cool completely. Break mixture into clusters. Store tightly covered. Makes about ½ pound.

Coffee Walnuts

1½ cups chopped walnuts
1 cup packed brown sugar
½ cup sugar
½ cup light cream
1 tablespoon instant coffee
   crystals
1 teaspoon vanilla

● Line a 9x5x3-inch loaf pan with foil, extending foil over edges of pan. Butter the foil; set pan aside.

● To toast the chopped walnuts, spread nuts in a single layer in a shallow baking pan. Toast nuts in a 350° oven about 10 minutes, stirring occasionally; keep nuts warm.

● Butter the sides of a heavy 1½-quart saucepan. In the saucepan combine brown sugar, sugar, cream, and coffee crystals. Cook over medium-high heat to boiling, stirring constantly with a wooden spoon to dissolve sugars. This should take about 4 minutes. Avoid splashing mixture on sides of pan. Carefully clip candy thermometer to side of pan.

● Cook over medium heat, stirring frequently, till thermometer registers 236°, soft-ball stage (see pages 10 and 11). Mixture should boil at a moderate, steady rate over the entire surface. Reaching soft-ball stage should take 6 to 8 minutes.

● Remove saucepan from heat; remove candy thermometer from saucepan. Add the vanilla. Beat gently with the wooden spoon for 2 minutes; stir in walnuts. Quickly turn the candy mixture into the prepared pan. Cool 10 minutes. Use foil to lift the candy out of the pan; cut the candy into about 1½-inch strips. Cut each strip into about 1½-inch triangles. Store tightly covered. Makes about 36 pieces.

Licorice, Marshmallows, and Gumdrops

Licorice, marshmallows, and gumdrops are three candies that people seldom realize they can make at home. Yet there is nothing mysterious about any of them!

Our licorice candy is flavored with anise extract. The herb anise was valued in early Greek, Roman, and Egyptian cultures for its reputed medicinal properties. Besides licorice candy, anise flavor is traditionally associated with special Christmas cookies, such as Springerle, and with some European yeast breads.

Marshmallows have an Egyptian origin and were first made from the sap of a tree—not an ingredient you'll need today! If you've never made marshmallows, you'll delight in seeing the sugar syrup transformed into springy marshmallows by combining the egg whites with the gelatin.

Commercial gumdrops are made from a binding ingredient called gum arabic, which gives the candy its familiar gelatinous texture. Our homemade gumdrops, which rely on pectin for their structure, have a fresh, chewy texture that cannot be matched!

Hard Licorice Drops

Add a few more drops of the anise extract for a stronger licorice flavor.

2 cups sugar
½ cup packed brown sugar
½ cup water
½ cup light corn syrup
¼ teaspoon anise extract
¼ teaspoon red food coloring
   or a very small amount
   of black paste food
   coloring

● Line a baking sheet with foil. Butter the foil; set baking sheet aside. Butter the sides of a heavy 2-quart saucepan. In the saucepan combine sugar, brown sugar, water, and corn syrup. Cook over medium-high heat to boiling, stirring constantly with a wooden spoon to dissolve sugars. This should take 6 to 8 minutes. Avoid splashing mixture on sides of pan. Carefully clip candy thermometer to side of pan.
● Cook over medium-high heat, stirring occasionally, till the thermometer registers 290°, soft-crack stage (see pages 10 and 11). Mixture should boil at a moderate, steady rate over the entire surface. Reaching soft-crack stage should take 30 to 35 minutes.
● Remove saucepan from heat; remove candy thermometer from saucepan. Immediately stir in the anise extract and the red or black food coloring. Drop the candy mixture from a teaspoon onto the prepared baking sheet, forming round patties.
● Let licorice drops stand about 30 minutes or till firm. Remove licorice drops from the baking sheet. Wrap each licorice drop in clear plastic wrap. Makes about 1 pound.

Chocolate Marshmallows

Sifted powdered sugar
2 envelopes unflavored
gelatin
½ cup cold water
1 cup sugar
1 cup light corn syrup
⅓ cup water
1 egg white
3 tablespoons unsweetened
cocoa powder

● Line bottom of a 9x9x2-inch baking pan with brown paper. Butter sides of pan and sprinkle with powdered sugar; set pan aside. Soften gelatin in the ½ cup cold water; set gelatin aside.

● Butter the sides of a heavy 1½-quart saucepan. In the pan combine sugar, corn syrup, and the ⅓ cup water. Cook over medium-high heat to boiling, stirring constantly with a wooden spoon to dissolve sugar. This should take about 10 minutes. Avoid splashing mixture on sides of pan. Carefully clip candy thermometer to side of pan.

● Cook over medium heat, without stirring, till thermometer registers 240°, soft-ball stage (see pages 10 and 11). Mixture should boil at a moderate, steady rate over the entire surface. Reaching soft-ball stage should take about 25 minutes. Remove saucepan from heat; remove thermometer from saucepan. Add gelatin mixture; stir till dissolved. Cool 10 minutes.

● Meanwhile, in a small mixer bowl beat egg white with an electric mixer till stiff peaks form. Transfer to a large mixer bowl. *Gradually* pour hot mixture in a thin stream (slightly less than ⅛-inch diameter) over egg white, beating on high speed; scrape bowl occasionally. This should take about 3 minutes. Add cocoa powder; beat on high speed, scraping bowl occasionally. When beaters are lifted, mixture should fall in a ribbon, but mound on itself and not disappear into remaining mixture. Final beating should take about 6 minutes.

● Turn into prepared pan; let stand about 1 hour. Dust with powdered sugar; invert onto a surface dusted with powdered sugar. Place a wet cloth over brown paper till moistened. Carefully peel off paper. Dust surface with powdered sugar. Using a wet knife, cut into 1-inch squares. Roll cut edges in powdered sugar. Store tightly covered. Makes 81 marshmallows.

Invert the pan of marshmallows onto a surface dusted with powdered sugar; carefully lift off the pan. Place a wet cloth over the brown paper. Let stand a few minutes till moistened. Carefully peel off the paper; dust the surface of the candy with powdered sugar.

Use a wet knife to cut the marshmallows into 1-inch squares. Roll the cut edges in powdered sugar so the candy doesn't stick together.

Orange Gumdrops

Our Taste Panel rated these homemade gumdrops outstanding. (Pictured on page 72.)

1 cup sugar
1 cup light corn syrup
¾ cup water
1 1¾-ounce package
    powdered fruit pectin
½ teaspoon baking soda
1½ teaspoons orange extract
1 teaspoon finely shredded
    orange peel
4 drops yellow food coloring
1 drop red food coloring
    Sugar

● Line a 9x5x3-inch loaf pan with foil, extending foil over edges of the pan. Butter the foil; set pan aside.

● Butter the sides of a heavy 1½-quart saucepan. In the saucepan combine the 1 cup sugar and the corn syrup. Cook over medium-high heat to boiling, stirring constantly with a wooden spoon to dissolve sugar. This should take about 10 minutes. Avoid splashing mixture on sides of pan. Carefully clip candy thermometer to side of pan.

● Cook over medium-high heat, stirring occasionally, till the thermometer registers 280°, soft-crack stage (see pages 10 and 11). Mixture should boil at a moderate, steady rate over the entire surface. Reaching soft-crack stage should take about 10 minutes.

● Meanwhile, in a heavy 2-quart saucepan combine water, pectin, and baking soda. (Mixture will be foamy.) Cook over high heat to boiling, stirring constantly. This should take about 2 minutes. Remove saucepan from heat; set saucepan aside.

● When sugar mixture has reached soft-crack stage, remove the saucepan from heat; remove candy thermometer from saucepan. Return pectin mixture to high heat; cook till mixture just begins to simmer. *Gradually* pour the hot sugar mixture in a thin stream (slightly less than ⅛-inch diameter) into the boiling pectin mixture, stirring constantly. This should take 1 to 2 minutes. Cook, stirring constantly, 1 minute more.

● Remove saucepan from heat. Stir in orange extract, orange peel, and yellow and red food colorings. Pour candy mixture into prepared pan. Let stand about 2 hours or till firm.

● When firm, use foil to lift candy out of pan. Use a buttered knife to cut candy into about ¾-inch squares. Roll squares in additional sugar. Store loosely covered. Makes about 72 pieces.

Cinnamon Gumdrops: Prepare Orange Gumdrops as directed above, *except* substitute 3 drops *oil of cinnamon* and 7 drops *red food coloring* for the orange extract, orange peel, and yellow and red food colorings.

Mint Gumdrops: Prepare Orange Gumdrops as directed above, *except* substitute ¾ teaspoon *mint extract* and 7 drops *green food coloring* for the orange extract, orange peel, and yellow and red food colorings.

Lemon Gumdrops: Prepare Orange Gumdrops as directed above, *except* substitute 1½ teaspoons *lemon extract,* 1 teaspoon finely shredded *lemon peel,* and 7 drops *yellow food coloring* for the orange extract, orange peel, and yellow and red food colorings.

Popcorn and Candy Bars

Popcorn and candy bars are two of America's most popular snacks. Where would Saturday afternoon matinees be without them!

American Indians introduced the settlers to corn that popped when it was heated. It soon became customary to use this popping corn as a breakfast cereal, sweetened with molasses and cream. From there, the idea of candied popcorn evolved by boiling together molasses and cream for a syrup used to pour over the popped corn.

The candy bar came along in the early 1900s. Later, as manufacturing methods improved during World War I, candy bars were mass-produced for the servicemen. Now, a large part of the candy market is in the familiar form of candy bars.

Sugared Popcorn

Make this sugar-coated popcorn on the range top.

⅓ cup unpopped popcorn
¼ cup water
3 tablespoons cooking oil
⅓ cup sugar
⅛ teaspoon ground cinnamon
  (optional)

● In a small bowl combine the unpopped popcorn and the water; set bowl aside. Pour the cooking oil into a heavy 3-quart saucepan. Add 2 or 3 kernels of unpopped popcorn; cover and cook over medium-high heat till you hear the kernels pop.
● Stir in sugar and, if desired, ground cinnamon. Carefully add the popcorn-water mixture.
● Cover and cook over medium-high heat till the popping slows, shaking the saucepan constantly. Quickly remove the saucepan from the heat to prevent the sugar from scorching.
● Immediately pour the popcorn into a large bowl. Store tightly covered. Makes about 6 cups.

Caramel Corn

Stir in some peanuts to make this oven caramel corn even more delicious! (Pictured on page 80.)

8 cups popped popcorn
   (about ⅓ to ½ cup
   unpopped)
¾ cup packed brown sugar
⅓ cup butter *or* margarine
3 tablespoons light corn
   syrup
¼ teaspoon baking soda
¼ teaspoon vanilla

● Remove all unpopped kernels from popped corn. Place popcorn in a greased 17x12x2-inch baking pan. Keep popcorn warm in a 300° oven while making caramel mixture.
● Butter the sides of a heavy 1½-quart saucepan. In the saucepan combine brown sugar, butter or margarine, and corn syrup. Cook over medium heat to boiling, stirring constantly with a wooden spoon to dissolve sugar. This should take 8 to 10 minutes. Avoid splashing mixture on sides of pan. Carefully clip candy thermometer to side of pan.
● Cook over medium heat, stirring occasionally, till thermometer registers 255°, hard-ball stage (see pages 10 and 11). Mixture should boil at a moderate, steady rate over the entire surface. Reaching hard-ball stage should take about 4 minutes.
● Remove saucepan from heat; remove candy thermometer from saucepan. Add baking soda and vanilla; stir till well combined. Pour caramel mixture over the popcorn; stir gently to coat popcorn. Bake in a 300° oven for 15 minutes; stir. Bake 5 minutes more. Turn popcorn mixture onto a large piece of foil. Cool completely. Break popcorn mixture into clusters. Store tightly covered. Makes about 9½ cups.

Apricot-Toffee Corn

Surprise popcorn lovers in your house with this buttery snack that's full of apricots and pecans.

8 cups popped popcorn
   (about ⅓ to ½ cup
   unpopped)
1 cup butter *or* margarine
1 cup sugar
3 tablespoons water
1 tablespoon light corn syrup
½ cup snipped dried apricots
½ cup coarsely chopped
   pecans
½ teaspoon vanilla

● Remove all unpopped kernels from popped corn. Place popcorn in a greased 17x12x2-inch baking pan. Keep popcorn warm in a 300° oven while making apricot mixture.
● Butter the sides of a heavy 2-quart saucepan. In the saucepan combine the 1 cup butter or margarine, sugar, water, and corn syrup. Cook over medium heat to boiling, stirring constantly with a wooden spoon to dissolve sugar. This should take 7 to 8 minutes. Avoid splashing mixture on sides of pan. Carefully clip candy thermometer to side of pan.
● Cook over medium heat, stirring occasionally, till thermometer registers 255°, hard-ball stage (see pages 10 and 11). Mixture should boil at a moderate, steady rate over the entire surface. Reaching hard-ball stage should take 10 to 15 minutes.
● Remove saucepan from heat; remove candy thermometer from saucepan. Quickly add snipped dried apricots, pecans, and vanilla; stir till well combined. Pour apricot mixture over the popcorn; stir gently to coat popcorn. Bake in a 300° oven for 15 minutes; stir. Bake 5 minutes more. Turn popcorn mixture onto a large piece of foil. Cool completely. Break popcorn mixture into clusters. Store tightly covered. Makes about 10 cups.

Molasses Gorp Popcorn Logs

If you don't have time to shape the popcorn mixture into logs, break it into clusters and serve.

12 cups popped popcorn
     (about ½ to ¾ cup
     unpopped)
 2 cups peanuts
 ½ cup candy-coated milk
     chocolate pieces
 ½ cup raisins
 1 cup sugar
 ½ cup water
 ½ cup light molasses
 ½ teaspoon salt

● Remove all unpopped kernels from popped corn. In a greased 17x12x2-inch baking pan combine popped corn, peanuts, chocolate pieces, and raisins. Set pan aside.

● Butter the sides of a heavy 3-quart saucepan. In the saucepan combine sugar, water, molasses, and salt. Cook over medium-high heat to boiling, stirring constantly with a wooden spoon to dissolve sugar. This should take about 5 minutes. Avoid splashing mixture on sides of pan. Carefully clip candy thermometer to side of pan.

● Cook over medium heat, stirring occasionally, till thermometer registers 250°, hard-ball stage (see pages 10 and 11). Mixture should boil at a moderate, steady rate over entire surface. Reaching hard-ball stage should take about 10 minutes.

● Remove saucepan from heat; remove candy thermometer from saucepan. Pour sugar mixture over the popcorn mixture; stir gently to coat the popcorn mixture. Cool till popcorn mixture can be handled easily. Use buttered hands to shape mixture into 3-inch logs, about 1½ inches in diameter. Wrap each log in clear plastic wrap. Makes about 36 logs.

Cinnamon Popcorn Balls

The thin layer of red candy coating is full of cinnamon flavor.

12 cups popped popcorn
     (about ½ to ¾ cup
     unpopped)
 1 cup sugar
 ⅔ cup water
 ⅓ cup red cinnamon candies
 1 tablespoon vinegar
 ¼ teaspoon salt
 1 *or* 2 drops oil of cinnamon
     (optional)

● Remove all unpopped kernels from popped corn. Place popcorn in a greased 17x12x2-inch baking pan. Keep popcorn warm in a 300° oven while making cinnamon mixture.

● Butter the sides of a heavy 1½-quart saucepan. In the saucepan combine sugar, water, red cinnamon candies, vinegar, and salt. Cook over medium-high heat to boiling, stirring constantly with a wooden spoon to dissolve sugar and cinnamon candies. This should take about 6 minutes. Avoid splashing mixture on sides of pan. Carefully clip candy thermometer to side of pan.

● Cook over medium heat, stirring occasionally, till thermometer registers 270°, soft-crack stage (see pages 10–11). Mixture should boil at a moderate, steady rate over the entire surface. Reaching soft-crack stage should take 20 to 25 minutes.

● Remove saucepan from heat; remove candy thermometer from saucepan. Stir in oil of cinnamon, if desired. Pour the cinnamon mixture over the popcorn; stir gently to coat the popcorn. Cool till the popcorn mixture can be handled easily. Use buttered hands to shape the mixture into 3-inch-diameter balls. Wrap each popcorn ball in clear plastic wrap. Makes about 10 popcorn balls.

Caramel Corn (see recipe, page 78)

Peanut Caramel Candy Bars

Coconut-Almond Candy Bars

Peanut-Caramel Candy Bars

Chewy caramel and chopped peanuts team up in these snack-size candy bars.

1 14-ounce package vanilla
   caramels
3 tablespoons butter *or*
   margarine
2 tablespoons milk
1 cup chopped peanuts
1½ pounds dipping chocolate *or*
   confectioner's coating

● Line an 8x8x2-inch baking pan with foil, extending foil over edges of pan. Butter the foil; set pan aside.

● In a heavy 1½-quart saucepan combine vanilla caramels, the 3 tablespoons butter or margarine, and milk. Cook over low heat, stirring occasionally, till caramels are melted. Stir in the chopped peanuts. Pour mixture into prepared pan.

● Chill about 1 hour or till firm. When firm, use the foil to lift candy out of the pan; cut candy into 2x1-inch rectangles.

● Melt the dipping chocolate or confectioner's coating (see dipping instructions on pages 18 and 19). Carefully dip the rectangles, one at a time, into the melted chocolate. Let excess chocolate drip off rectangles.

● Place the dipped rectangles on a baking sheet lined with waxed paper till dry. Store tightly covered in a cool, dry place. Makes 32 candy bars.

Coconut-Almond Candy Bars

Deep, rich chocolate and creamy coconut centers combine for a mouth-watering treat.

3½ cups sifted powdered sugar
1 3-ounce package cream
   cheese, softened
1 teaspoon vanilla
1½ cups coconut
50 blanched whole
   almonds (about ⅓ cup)
1½ pounds dipping chocolate *or*
   confectioner's coating

● Butter a 12x9-inch piece of foil; set foil aside. In a small bowl combine powdered sugar, softened cream cheese, and vanilla. Stir in the coconut.

● Turn coconut mixture onto the buttered foil. Pat coconut mixture into a 10x5-inch rectangle. Cut the mixture into 2x1-inch rectangles. Press 2 blanched whole almonds into the top of each rectangle.

● Melt the dipping chocolate or confectioner's coating (see dipping instructions on pages 18 and 19). Carefully dip the rectangles, one at a time, into the melted chocolate. Let excess chocolate drip off rectangles.

● Place the dipped rectangles on a baking sheet lined with waxed paper till dry. Store tightly covered in a cool, dry place. Makes 25 candy bars.

Caramallow Candy Bars

½ cup sugar
¼ cup butter *or* margarine
¼ cup light cream
2 cups sifted powdered sugar
1 cup tiny marshmallows
¼ cup semisweet chocolate
    pieces
1½ cups vanilla caramels
    (about 34)
2 tablespoons butter *or*
    margarine
1 tablespoon milk
1½ pounds dipping chocolate *or*
    confectioner's coating

● Line an 8x8x2-inch baking pan with foil, extending foil over edges of pan. Butter the foil; set pan aside.
● In a heavy 2-quart saucepan combine sugar, the ¼ cup butter, and cream. Cook over medium heat to boiling, stirring constantly to dissolve sugar. This should take about 8 minutes.
● Cook over medium heat, stirring occasionally, for 3 minutes. Mixture should boil at a moderate, steady rate over entire surface. Remove pan from heat. Add powdered sugar, marshmallows, and chocolate pieces; stir till well combined and chocolate is melted. Pour mixture into prepared pan. Cool 20 minutes.
● Meanwhile, in a heavy 1½-quart saucepan combine caramels, the 2 tablespoons butter, and milk. Cook over low heat, stirring occasionally, till caramels are melted. Pour caramel mixture over chocolate layer in baking pan. Chill about 1 hour or till firm. When firm, use foil to lift candy out of pan. Invert candy so chocolate layer is on top. Cut into 2x1-inch rectangles.
● Melt dipping chocolate or confectioner's coating (see dipping instructions on pages 18 and 19). Dip rectangles, one at a time, into melted chocolate. Let excess chocolate drip off rectangles. Place on a baking sheet lined with waxed paper till dry. Store tightly covered in a cool, dry place. Makes 32 candy bars.

Fruit and Nut Candy Bars

Even without the chocolate, these candy bars make good eating. To store, simply wrap them individually in clear plastic wrap and refrigerate.

⅓ cup sugar
¼ cup light cream
¼ cup butter *or* margarine
1 3-ounce package cream
    cheese, softened
2 cups sifted powdered sugar
1 cup chopped mixed dried
    fruits
½ cup chopped nuts
½ teaspoon vanilla
1½ pounds dipping chocolate *or*
    confectioner's coating

● Line an 8x8x2-inch baking pan with foil, extending foil over edges of pan. Butter the foil; set pan aside.
● In a heavy 2-quart saucepan combine the sugar, light cream, and the ¼ cup butter or margarine. Cook over medium heat to boiling, stirring constantly to dissolve the sugar. This should take about 8 minutes.
● Cook over medium heat, stirring occasionally, for 3 minutes. Mixture should boil at a moderate, steady rate over the entire surface. Remove pan from heat. Add cream cheese; stir till smooth. Add powdered sugar, dried fruits, nuts, and vanilla; stir till well combined. Spread mixture into the prepared pan. Chill about 1 hour or till firm. When firm, use foil to lift candy out of pan; cut candy into 2x1-inch rectangles.
● Melt the dipping chocolate or confectioner's coating (see dipping instructions on pages 18 and 19). Carefully dip the rectangles, one at a time, into the melted chocolate. Let excess coating drip off rectangles. Place the dipped rectangles on a baking sheet lined with waxed paper till dry. Store tightly covered in refrigerator. Makes 32 candy bars.

Dipped Favorites

Mastering the art of candy-making would be incomplete without learning how to dip your favorite candy centers and fruits into chocolate. Many beginners are leary of this area of candy-making. But the process simply takes time and patience. With a steady hand and a little bit of practice, anyone can make irresistible, professional-looking dipped specialties.

Many professional candy-makers have developed a special signature for their dipped candies, and you can too. Some of the most elegant designs are created by lightly touching the surface of the candy with the tines of a fork, or simply leaving a trail of coating over the surface to form a raised pattern.

So, even if you're a beginner, don't be afraid to try dipping your favorite confections. You, too, can make an impressive array of chocolate-coated candies.

Fancy Liqueur Chocolates

Delicately flavored with liqueur, then dipped in chocolate, these candies look and taste like expensive purchased chocolates. (Pictured on page 51.)

  2 **cups sugar**
  ½ **cup water**
  ¼ **cup light cream**
  1 **tablespoon light corn syrup**
  2 **tablespoons Amaretto** *or* **coffee liqueur**
  1 **pound dipping chocolate** *or* **confectioner's coating**

● Butter the sides of a heavy 2-quart saucepan. In the saucepan combine sugar, water, cream, and light corn syrup. Cook over medium-high heat to boiling, stirring constantly with a wooden spoon to dissolve sugar. This should take 5 to 6 minutes. Avoid splashing mixture on sides of pan. Carefully clip candy thermometer to side of saucepan.

● Cook over medium-low heat, stirring occasionally, till the thermometer registers 240°, soft-ball stage (see pages 10 and 11). The mixture should boil at a moderate, steady rate over the entire surface. Reaching soft-ball stage should take 15 to 20 minutes.

● Remove saucepan from heat. Cool, without stirring, to lukewarm (110°). This should take about 45 minutes. Remove candy thermometer from saucepan. Add Amaretto or coffee liqueur; beat with the wooden spoon till candy becomes creamy and slightly stiff. This should take about 10 minutes.

● Shape candy into 1-inch balls; place balls on a baking sheet lined with waxed paper. Let the balls stand at room temperature about 20 minutes or till dry.

● Melt the dipping chocolate or confectioner's coating (see dipping instructions on pages 18 and 19). Carefully dip balls into melted chocolate. Let excess chocolate drip off balls. Place the dipped balls on a baking sheet lined with waxed paper till dry. Store tightly covered in a cool, dry place. Makes about 40 pieces.

Fancy Vanilla Chocolates: Prepare Fancy Liqueur Chocolates as directed above, *except* substitute 2 teaspoons *vanilla* for the Amaretto or coffee liqueur.

Chocolate-Covered Cherries

For a nontraditional look, dip these candies into vanilla-flavored coating.

60 maraschino cherries with
  stems (about two
  10-ounce jars)
3 tablespoons butter *or*
  margarine, softened
3 tablespoons light corn
  syrup
2 cups sifted powdered sugar
1 pound dipping chocolate *or*
  confectioner's coating

● Drain cherries thoroughly on paper towels for several hours. In a small mixing bowl combine softened butter or margarine and corn syrup. Stir in sifted powdered sugar; knead mixture till smooth (chill mixture if it is too soft to handle).

● Shape about ½ *teaspoon* of the powdered sugar mixture around *each* cherry. Place coated cherries upright on a baking sheet lined with waxed paper; chill till firm.

● Melt the dipping chocolate or confectioner's coating (see dipping instructions on pages 18 and 19). Holding the cherries by the stems, dip cherries, one at a time, into the melted chocolate; spoon chocolate over the cherries to coat. (Be sure to completely seal the cherries in chocolate; otherwise, cherry juice may leak out after the chocolate has set.) Let excess chocolate drip off cherries. Place the dipped cherries, stem side up, on a baking sheet lined with waxed paper.

● Chill the dipped cherries till chocolate is firm. Place cherries in a tightly covered container. Let stand (ripen) in the refrigerator for 1 to 2 weeks before serving. (Ripening is necessary to allow the powdered sugar mixture around cherries to soften and liquefy.) Store tightly covered in refrigerator. Makes 60 pieces.

Chocolate-Covered Liqueur Cherries: Prepare Chocolate-Covered Cherries as directed above, *except* drain cherries, reserving 1¼ cups of the *cherry liquid.* Place the reserved liquid in a small saucepan and bring to boiling; remove from heat. Stir in ½ cup *Amaretto, coffee liqueur, or crème de cacao*; stir in the cherries. Cover the saucepan and let stand overnight. Drain the cherries thoroughly on paper towels for several hours. Continue as directed above.

Chocolate-Dipped Fruit

Arrange the pieces of dipped fruit in colored individual paper cups for a pretty presentation.

5 cups maraschino cherries,
  canned mandarin orange
  sections, fresh
  strawberries, *and/or* dried
  apricots
1 pound dipping chocolate *or*
  confectioner's coating

● Drain the cherries, mandarin orange sections, and/or fresh strawberries thoroughly on paper towels for several hours.

● Melt the dipping chocolate or confectioner's coating (see dipping instructions on pages 18 and 19). Holding fruit with your fingers, dip a portion of the fruit into the melted chocolate. (Or, to completely cover the fruit, drop the fruit, one piece at a time, into the melted chocolate. Use a fork to lift the fruit out of the chocolate.) Let excess chocolate drip off fruit. Place the dipped fruit on a baking sheet lined with waxed paper till dry. Serve the dipped fruit the same day it is dipped. Makes about 2½ pounds.

Three-Layer Diamonds

Layers of chocolate, candied fruit, and almonds are encased in chocolate.

Sifted powdered sugar
½ cup semisweet chocolate
   pieces
2 tablespoons butter *or*
   margarine
4 cups sifted powdered sugar
4 teaspoons light cream
   or milk
¼ teaspoon vanilla
¾ cup finely chopped mixed
   candied fruits
¾ cup slivered almonds
1 egg white
⅛ teaspoon almond extract
1 pound dipping chocolate *or*
   confectioner's coating

● Sprinkle powdered sugar on a baking sheet lined with waxed paper; set aside. In a small saucepan melt semisweet chocolate pieces and butter or margarine over low heat; stir constantly.

● Remove pan from heat. Stir in *1 cup* of the powdered sugar; stir in cream and vanilla. Add *¾ cup* of the powdered sugar; stir till well combined. If necessary, add a few drops additional cream to make mixture pliable. Turn onto prepared baking sheet; pat into a 9x6-inch rectangle.

● Sprinkle the chocolate rectangle with the candied fruits. Press fruits lightly into chocolate mixture; set mixture aside.

● Place the slivered almonds in a blender container or a food processor bowl; cover and blend till finely ground. In a small mixer bowl combine ground almonds, ¾ cup of the powdered sugar, egg white, and almond extract. Beat with an electric mixer on low speed till well combined. Add the remaining 1½ cups powdered sugar; beat on low speed till smooth.

● Sprinkle powdered sugar on a piece of waxed paper. Turn almond mixture onto the waxed paper; cover with a second piece of waxed paper. Roll mixture into a 9x6-inch rectangle. Remove top piece of paper; invert almond mixture onto candied fruits. Remove waxed paper. Lightly press layers together. Chill for 2 to 3 hours.

● Cut candy lengthwise into eight ¾-inch strips. Cut diagonally across strips at ¾-inch intervals, forming about 1½x¾-inch diamond-shape pieces. Melt dipping chocolate or confectioner's coating (see dipping instructions on pages 18 and 19). Dip pieces into melted chocolate. Let excess chocolate drip off pieces. Let stand till dry. Store tightly covered in a cool, dry place. Makes about 80 pieces.

Assembling candy layers
Roll the almond mixture into a 9x6-inch rectangle between two pieces of waxed paper. Remove the top piece of waxed paper. Use the bottom piece of waxed paper to lift and invert the almond mixture onto the candied fruits. Remove the waxed paper. Lightly press the candy layers together in center and around edges so the layers will stick together when the pieces are dipped.

SHORT AND SNAPPY CANDIES

When you find yourself short of time, yet you yearn for some homemade candies, consider such delicious recipes as Rocky Road and Peanut Butter Cups, which don't require a watchful eye or constant temperature testing. And we're also sure you'll like the small number of ingredients and preparation steps in these shortcut candy recipes.

But just a word of caution: You'll soon discover that these candies are as easy to eat as they are to make!

Microwave Peanut Clusters

If you don't own a microwave, you can make these candies by melting the coating and chocolate in a saucepan on top of the range. Use low heat and stir constantly. (Pictured on page 91.)

½ pound vanilla-flavored
    confectioner's coating,
    cut up
1 6-ounce package (1 cup)
    semisweet chocolate
    pieces
2 cups peanuts

● Place the vanilla-flavored confectioner's coating and the chocolate pieces in a 2½-quart nonmetal bowl. Cook, uncovered, in a countertop microwave oven on 100% power (HIGH) about 2½ minutes or just till the mixture becomes smooth when stirred. Stir in the peanuts.

● Drop peanut mixture from a teaspoon onto a baking sheet lined with waxed paper. Chill about 30 minutes or till firm. Store tightly covered in refrigerator. Makes about 36 pieces.

Microwave Butterscotch Peanut Clusters: Prepare Microwave Peanut Clusters as directed above, *except* substitute ½ pound cut-up *butterscotch-flavored confectioner's coating* for the vanilla-flavored confectioner's coating.

Easy Mint Patties

A special occasion coming up? To simplify last-minute preparations, make these mints ahead and freeze them. Before serving the mints, let them stand at room temperature for several hours.

⅓ cup light corn syrup
¼ cup butter *or* margarine,
    softened
1 teaspoon peppermint
    extract
4¾ cups sifted powdered sugar
    (about 1 pound)
1 *or* 2 drops desired food
    coloring

● In a mixing bowl combine light corn syrup, softened butter or margarine, and peppermint extract. Add powdered sugar, about 1 cup at a time, stirring till well combined.

● Stir desired food coloring into mixture. (Or, divide mixture in half and stir a different food coloring into each portion.)

● Shape candy mixture into 1-inch balls. Place the balls 2 inches apart on a baking sheet lined with waxed paper. Gently flatten each ball with the tines of a fork. Let candy stand at room temperature about 3 hours or till dry. Store tightly covered in refrigerator. Makes about 56 patties.

Peanutty Fudge Rounds

Rolling chocolate around a peanut center creates a favorite flavor combination.

¾ cup creamy peanut butter
2 tablespoons butter *or* margarine, softened
1 cup sifted powdered sugar
1 tablespoon milk
1 teaspoon vanilla
½ cup chopped peanuts
1 12-ounce package (2 cups) semisweet chocolate pieces
½ cup *sweetened condensed milk*

● In a medium mixing bowl stir together peanut butter and softened butter or margarine. Add powdered sugar, milk, and vanilla, stirring till well combined. Stir in peanuts. Shape the mixture into two 10-inch rolls; set rolls aside.

● In a small saucepan combine chocolate pieces and sweetened condensed milk. Cook over low heat, stirring constantly, till melted and smooth.

● Remove saucepan from heat; turn chocolate mixture onto waxed paper. Divide the mixture in half. Working on waxed paper, pat each half into a 10x4-inch rectangle. Place *one* peanut roll in the center of *each* chocolate rectangle. Use the waxed paper to help bring the chocolate mixture up and around each of the peanut rolls; press seams to seal.

● Wrap candy rolls in waxed paper or clear plastic wrap; chill for 2 to 3 hours or till firm. Unwrap and carefully cut rolls into ¼-inch slices. Store tightly covered. Makes about 80 slices.

Rolling chocolate around the peanut rolls
Place one of the peanut rolls in the center of one of the 10x4-inch chocolate rectangles. Use the waxed paper to help bring the chocolate mixture up and around the peanut roll; press the chocolate edges together to seal. Repeat with the remaining chocolate mixture and peanut roll.

Wrap rolls and chill till firm. Then unwrap and carefully cut rolls into ¼-inch slices.

Caramel Snappers

Topping pecan clusters with a mound of melted caramel and chocolate creates a chewy candy that's rich in flavor. (Pictured on page 91.)

90 pecan halves
    (about 1½ cups)
½ of a 14-ounce package
    (about 25) vanilla
    caramels
1 tablespoon water
½ cup semisweet chocolate
    pieces

● To toast pecan halves, spread nuts in a single layer in a shallow baking pan. Toast the nuts in a 350° oven about 10 minutes, stirring occasionally.

● Line a baking sheet with foil. Butter the foil. On prepared baking sheet arrange toasted pecans in groups of three, placing flat side of pecan halves down; set baking sheet aside.

● In a heavy 1-quart saucepan combine the caramels and water. Cook over low heat, stirring constantly, till caramels are melted and smooth.

● Remove saucepan from heat. Drop about *1 teaspoon* of the melted caramel mixture onto *each* group of pecans. Let stand about 20 minutes or till caramel mixture is firm.

● In a small saucepan heat the chocolate pieces over low heat, stirring constantly, till melted and smooth. Remove saucepan from heat. With a narrow metal spatula spread a small amount of the melted chocolate over the top of each caramel center. Let stand till firm. When firm, remove candy from the baking sheet. Store tightly covered. Makes 30 pieces.

Butterscotch Brickle Squares

Vanilla-flavored coating tops a smooth, rich butterscotch base for a two-tone candy.

1 6-ounce package (1 cup)
    butterscotch pieces
¼ cup butter *or* margarine
2 cups sifted powdered sugar
½ cup almond brickle pieces
2 tablespoons milk
6 ounces vanilla-flavored
    confectioner's coating,
    cut up
¼ cup slivered almonds,
    toasted

● Line an 8x8x2-inch baking pan with foil, extending foil over edges of pan. Butter the foil; set pan aside.

● In a 2-quart saucepan heat butterscotch pieces and the ¼ cup butter or margarine over low heat, stirring constantly, till melted and smooth. Remove saucepan from heat. Add the powdered sugar, almond brickle pieces, and milk; stir till well combined. Pat butterscotch mixture into the prepared pan.

● In a small saucepan heat vanilla-flavored confectioner's coating over low heat, stirring constantly, till melted and smooth. Carefully pour the melted coating over the butterscotch layer; sprinkle with almonds.

● Chill about 1 hour or till firm. When firm, use foil to lift candy out of pan; cut candy into 1-inch squares. Store tightly covered. Makes 64 pieces.

Easy Fudge

In a hurry? This recipe is faster than traditional fudge recipes.

3¾ cups sifted powdered
sugar
½ cup unsweetened cocoa
powder
½ cup nonfat dry milk powder
½ cup butter *or* margarine
¼ cup water
½ cup chopped nuts

● Line an 8x8x2-inch baking pan with foil, extending foil over edges of pan. Butter the foil; set pan aside.
● Sift together powdered sugar and unsweetened cocoa powder into a large mixing bowl. (If sugar mixture seems lumpy, sift it again.) Set sugar mixture aside.
● In a small saucepan combine dry milk powder, the ½ cup butter or margarine, and water. Cook over medium heat just to boiling, stirring constantly to melt butter or margarine.
● Remove pan from heat. Stir the melted butter mixture into the powdered sugar mixture. Add the chopped nuts, stirring till well combined.
● Turn fudge into the prepared pan. While fudge is warm, score it into 1-inch squares. Chill several hours or till firm. When firm, use foil to lift candy out of the pan; cut candy into squares. Store tightly covered. Makes 64 pieces or about 1½ pounds.

Rocky Road

Add some extra color to this candy by using colored marshmallows.

2 8-ounce bars milk
chocolate, cut up
3 cups tiny
marshmallows
¾ cup coarsely chopped
walnuts

● Line an 8x8x2-inch baking pan with foil, extending foil over edges of pan. Butter the foil; set pan aside.
● In a medium saucepan heat the milk chocolate over low heat, stirring constantly, till melted and smooth. Remove saucepan from heat. Stir in marshmallows and chopped walnuts. Spread mixture into prepared pan.
● Chill candy mixture about 30 minutes or till firm. When firm, use foil to lift candy out of pan; cut candy into 1-inch squares. Store tightly covered. Makes 64 pieces.

Rocky Road

Caramel Snappers
(see recipe, page 89)

Microwave Peanut Clusters
(see recipe, page 87)

Bourbon Balls

Letting these bourbon balls stand for a few days before serving allows the bourbon to blend with the other ingredients.

1 cup finely crushed vanilla
    wafers (about 22 wafers)
1 cup sifted powdered sugar
⅔ cup chopped walnuts
¼ cup chopped candied
    cherries
2 tablespoons unsweetened
    cocoa powder
3 tablespoons bourbon
1 tablespoon water
1½ teaspoons light corn syrup
    Sifted powdered sugar

● In a mixing bowl combine crushed vanilla wafers, the 1 cup powdered sugar, walnuts, candied cherries, and cocoa powder. Stir in bourbon, water, and light corn syrup till well combined. Chill the mixture about 30 minutes.

● Shape the mixture into 1-inch balls. Place balls in an airtight container; let the balls stand (ripen) for 2 to 3 days. Before serving the balls, roll them in additional sifted powdered sugar. Makes about 24 pieces.

Peanut Butter Cups

These peanut butter treats surrounded by chocolate are slightly larger than the ones you buy.

1 6-ounce package (1 cup)
    semisweet chocolate
    pieces
½ cup milk chocolate pieces
½ cup chunk-style peanut
    butter
2 tablespoons chopped
    peanuts

● Using one 12-cup muffin pan or two 6-cup muffin pans, line *eight* muffin cups with paper bake cups; set pan or pans aside.

● In a small saucepan heat semisweet chocolate pieces and milk chocolate pieces over low heat, stirring constantly, till melted and smooth.

● Remove saucepan from heat. In another small saucepan heat the peanut butter over low heat, stirring constantly, till melted. Remove saucepan from heat.

● Pour about *1 tablespoon* melted chocolate into *each* paper bake cup; chill about 5 minutes or till chocolate is firm. Pour about *1 tablespoon* melted peanut butter over the firm chocolate in *each* paper bake cup; chill candy about 5 minutes more or till peanut butter is firm.

● Pour the remaining melted chocolate evenly over the peanut butter layer in *each* paper bake cup, spreading the chocolate to cover the peanut butter. Sprinkle each with chopped peanuts.

● Chill candy about 10 minutes more or till firm. Store tightly covered in the refrigerator. Makes 8 pieces.

Swirled Almond Candy

Swirling the chocolate into the vanilla-flavored coating makes this easy candy look fancy.

1 cup whole almonds
1 6-ounce package (1 cup) semisweet chocolate pieces
1 pound vanilla-flavored confectioner's coating, cut up

● To toast whole almonds, spread nuts in a single layer in a shallow baking pan. Toast nuts in a 350° oven for 8 to 10 minutes, stirring occasionally.

● Line a baking sheet with foil; set baking sheet aside. In a small saucepan heat chocolate pieces over low heat, stirring constantly, till melted and smooth. Remove pan from heat.

● In a 2-quart saucepan heat the confectioner's coating over low heat, stirring constantly, till melted and smooth. Remove saucepan from heat. Stir in toasted almonds.

● Pour the melted coating mixture onto the prepared baking sheet. Spread coating mixture to about ⅜-inch thickness; drizzle with the melted chocolate. *Gently* zigzag a narrow metal spatula through the mixtures to swirl slightly.

● Let stand several hours or till firm. (Or, chill about 30 minutes or till firm.) When firm, use foil to lift candy from the baking sheet; break candy into pieces. Store tightly covered. Makes about 1¼ pounds.

Easy Cherry Chocolates

Using a frosting mix helps make this candy simple to fix.

1 12-ounce package (2 cups) semisweet chocolate pieces
½ cup finely chopped nuts
3 tablespoons milk
2 tablespoons butter *or* margarine
1 package creamy cherry frosting mix (for 2-layer cake)

● Line an 11x7x1½-inch baking pan with foil, extending foil over edges of pan; set pan aside.

● In a small saucepan heat the chocolate pieces over low heat, stirring constantly, till melted and smooth. Remove saucepan from heat; stir in chopped nuts. Spread *half* of the chocolate mixture into the prepared baking pan; freeze about 10 minutes or till chocolate is firm.

● In a medium saucepan combine milk and butter or margarine. Cook over low heat, stirring occasionally, till butter or margarine is melted. Remove saucepan from heat. Add cherry frosting mix; stir till well combined. Spread frosting mixture over the firm chocolate layer. Spread the remaining chocolate mixture over the frosting layer. (If necessary, reheat chocolate mixture over low heat to make it spreadable.)

● Freeze about 10 minutes more or till chocolate is firm. When firm, use foil to lift candy out of pan; cut candy into 1-inch squares. Store tightly covered. Makes 77 pieces.

Index